THE MEXICAN ADAPTATION IN AMERICAN CALIFORNIA 1846–1875
(1955) University of California

WITHDRAWI

RICHARD H. MOREFIELD

Reprinted in 1971 by R and E Research
Associates, publishers and distributors of
ethnic studies. 4843 Mission Street, San
Francisco, California 94112 and 18581 Mc
Farland Avenue, Saratoga, California 95070
Editor: Adam S. Eterovich
Publisher: Robert D. Reed

Library of Congress
Card Catalog No.

72-147291

PREFACE

The history of the Mexicans in American California has usually been written in terms of race prejudice, violence, and bloodshed. In the following pages I have seemingly overlooked this story of bitter race relations in California. The story of persecution and violence is well known, however, and those who wish can find ample examples elsewhere. A preoccupation with those examples, however, can only give one viewpoint to the history of the Mexicans in California. This viewpoint is best typified by the views of the best known author on race relations in California:

> For over a hundred years, two cultural traditions--the Spanish-Mexican and the Anglo-American--have been in conflict in Southern California. In other areas of the Southwest Anglos, Hispanos, and Indians have long since achieved a measure of mutual respect and accommodation, but in Southern California, the conflict has been sharp and continuous . . .[1]
>
> This conflict is likely to continue until some fusion of the cultures takes place. . . These tensions will persist until the dominant group is prepared to accept the concept of bi-culturality, that is, until it is willing to let the Mexican alone, to treat him with respect, to recognize his equality, and to sanction the free use of the Spanish language and whatever other cultural traits may survive.[2]

There is another viewpoint of the history of the Mexicans in California--a viewpoint which I believe is equally true and even more important--which to date has not been set down. This concerns the successful assimilation of the Mexicans into American society. It is my belief that closer attention to this overlooked aspect will show the way to a better understanding of present day cultural problems.

History, to me, is not just a chronicle of facts; it is a conscious effort to find

---

[1] Carey McWilliams, Southern California Country, An Island on the Land (New York: Duel, Sloan and Pierce, 1946), p. 49.

[2] Ibid., pp. 320-1.

wisdom; and wisdom is the ability to organize knowledge in the mind in conformity with reality. Unfortunately there is no easy road to this goal; it is necessary to adapt subjective judgments to agree with what actually is. A start has to be made somewhere, however, and perhaps the best beginning is a frank evaluation of one's own motives and feelings.

What I have attempted is to view the areas of group contact between the Americans and the Mexicans in California in the first generation after the area was ceded to the United States. I have looked for successful attempts at assimilation in the hope that success in the past might help lead to similar success in the future. I am optimistic enough to believe that it is possible; I am idealistic enough to want it to come about.

TABLE OF CONTENTS

INTRODUCTION

The cultural heritage of the United States has been enriched by the constant flow, until comparatively recent times, of large numbers of immigrants whose cultural backgrounds differed from the here dominant Protestant Anglo-Saxon culture. In the process of economic, political and social assimilation these groups have given new roots and new vitality to our culture.

Each new addition to the American melting pot has had special assimilation problems, even though the general pattern is similar. In the Pacific South-West, the Mexican racial group has had a problem similar only to that of the American Indian: they were settled on the land when the Yankee came. In California the Mexican had established a political, economic and social system based on their cultural background and economic necessities. The question facing the Mexican and the Anglo-Saxon when the territory was transferred to the United States was the position these Mexican systems would play in the new "American" California.

The tremendous influx of population brought on by the gold rush completely destroyed any chance of the Mexican culture playing a prominent role in California. Despite the early fears of many Anglo-Saxons, in a few years it was soon clear that by weight of numbers alone, the Mexican culture in California would be submerged in the Protestant Anglo-Saxon Culture of the United States. Only in the southern portion of the state, where the gold rush did not destroy the large rancho, was there any hope of the Mexican culture contributing a major portion to the California scene. The story of the struggle of the first generation of Mexicans to become assimilated is largely the story of whether or not the Mexican heritage would be of major importance in at least one portion of the state.

1

CHAPTER I

HEWERS OF WOOD AND DRAWERS OF WATER:

MEXICANS IN THE MINES OF CALIFORNIA: 1848-1855

When the Mexican territory of Alta California was conquered by the Americans and finally ceded by the Treaty of Guadalupe, the first thought of the Americans in the new territory was to make it safe and secure for Americans and American institutions. Despite the comparative ease in which the land was wrestled from Mexico, a feeling grew that the Mexicans were a threat by their very numbers. As one early pioneer put it:

> . . . the authorities. . . made it an aim everywhere and particularly here in San Francisco, to build up a community that would overawe the Mexican population of the entire territory, anc create such an interest on the other side that the country could never go back to Mexico. The tendency of all their acts was in that direction--throwing out great inducements for people to come here who would be anything else but Mexican.[1]

The discovery of gold settled very quickly the problem of creating an interest for California. There would be little chance of California's ever going back to Mexico; and the problem of the military governors of California was changed slightly to become the problem which today is still unsolved; what is to be the place of the Mexican and the Mexican culture in California society?

It is impossible to deny that the long tradition of the Black Legend, the difference in language, even the relatively simple matter of difference of appearance, all did not have an effect in causing the troubles in the Gold Fields and

> . . . The old anti-Spanish prejudice of the Southwest. . . worked against them in California. . . More often, however, race prejudice. . . led the rougher element of a mining camp, many of whom were likely to be foreigners themselves, to seize the claims which the Mexicans or Chileans had opened up, and drive the latter away from the community. . .[2]

An attempt will be made to show, however, that the main cause in this period was economic. When it was to the economic advantage of the mining community to have a large foreign (principally Mexican or Spanish speaking) population, this population was welcomed. But when these groups were in competition with the American miners for claims or jobs, they were unwelcome, and consequently discriminated against.

A definition should be given for discrimination. The period was one of lynch law and violence; and although it has been generally accepted that the foreigner--especially the Mexican--had a more difficult time in obtaining justice,[3] it is hard to say that this man at this time was hung or punished because of prejudice. Americans as well as foreigners suffered mistreatment at the hands of mobs in this period. An attempt has been made, therefore, to find those cases where action was made over a period of time in order to discover those incidents in which a policy, rather than an example, of discrimination could be shown.

In 1848 the position of the Mexican in the gold fields was decided by two factors. First the majority of the Mexicans in California in the first year of the gold rush were native Californians, who could become citizens of the United States by the Treaty of Guadalupe. They were quick to point out to any zealous Yankee that they were just as much a citizen as he was, and had just as much right to the riches of the public domain.[4] Secondly, the only large number of people in California in 1848 who knew anything about mining were the Sonorans. These Mexicans, who had learned the skills in the mines of northern Mexico, were the teachers of the first miners in California.[5] The prestige and value of their instruction made them welcome the first year. It did not take long for the first troubles to begin, but they were on a small scale until the winter of 1849-50. The first year in the mines, then, was one of little trouble. The average Californians who came in 1848 came in parties of several rancheros, with servants, and possibly even a group of Indians to do the actual digging. They may have had an American in the Party. They went back to their rancho when the dry season of 1849 came, and may or may not have returned later in 1849.[6] Despite the money that they may have made in the mines, some of them were disappointed. As Augustin Janssens recalled in his memoirs, the disappointments were caused by the occasional trouble with the poorer element of society who flocked to the mines, the troubles with the hostile Indians, and the temptation that gold had on the Indian servants that he brought with him to work the gold placers.

> We ran many dangers, and had several struggles. Finally all was settled amiacably--after so much work and so much danger in our labors--without obtaining but very little gold, because the Indians robbed me of all the nuggets they found.[7]

At the beginning of the winter of 1849-50 the feeling was that the settled and peaceful times of the previous year would continue; it was felt that the threads could be picked up where they had been left off at the end of the past season. The mines continued to be the place where the young son of the impoverished family of la gente de razon could recoup the family fortune[8] or where the pioneer who had lost his savings in a poor business transaction could remake his fortune in three months in the gold fields.[9] But it was soon obvious that there had been a change in the mines and in the attitude of the Americans. A few of the Californians, seeing this change, gave up the idea of going back to the mines and settled down to make their living in the ranchos.[10] Others went on to the mines and became enmeshed in this struggle with the Americans. For the mines were filling up with new arrivals and

> Nine tenths of the new arrivals were Americans, who resorted... in the first instance to the Chileans and Mexicans for instruction and information, which they gave them with careful alacrity; but as soon as Jonathan got an inkling of the system, with peculiar bad taste and ingenerous feeling, he organized a crusade against these obliging strangers... in fact, the Yankee regarded every man but a native American as an interloper, who had no right to come to California and pick up the gold of "free and enlighted citizens."[11]

Where previously the troubles in the mines

> had not passed being shouts, shots into the air, and drunken threats, and finally everything calmed down and... (they)... returned to continue... (their)... work, although some of the weaker had been despoiled of their claims by the stronger...[12]

now the troubles were going to be more serious and more complex. As more and more people poured into the gold fields, the troubles began to grow. Especially in the southern diggings, where the Mexicans were in the largest numbers and the lack of water during most of the year made good claims with water more desirable, the period of good feelings in 1849 was of short duration.[13] In the latter part of July and early August the feeling against the foreigners grew, but no action was yet taken.[14] By the end of September it was being advertised that "none but Americans allowed" on the North and Middle Forks of the Stanislaus River[15]..but still there was no violence. By this time Mexicans were being eased out of diggings which they developed. At Sherlocks Diggings in Mariposa a group of Mexicans who had worked the diggings on shares with the discoverer were run off by the Americans when Sherlock went prospecting in the mountains.[16] One of the first outbreaks of violence occurred in the Calaveras Diggings about fifty miles from Stockton at the very end of 1849 and the first few days of 1850. At the beginning of the rainy season a group of Americans had selected a location on the river and erected cabins in preparation for the winter. The area had been a "dry digging" worked by Chileans and other foreigners during the summer. Early in December a group of Chileans appeared and started to work in the area. A meeting of the Americans was held and a judge and military captain were elected, who told the Chileans to leave within fifteen days, as they were not American citizens. A group of them remained about eight miles away and "abused and drove off three or four Americans who attempted to dig in the neighborhood." At the end of the fifteen day period the Chileans were brought before the judge and fined an ounce of gold and told to leave the area by Christmas day. The Chileans lodged a complaint of robbery and extortion with the authorities in Stockton and obtained a writ of arrest. No Americans could be found to enforce the writ, so the Chileans undertook to execute it. On the night of the 27th, a party of about 80 Chileans fell upon the Americans, killing two and wounding four in the struggle. They took the prisoners to Stanislaus--eight miles away--to an alcalde named Scullion whom they expected to accompany them to Stockton. When the alcalde refused to have anything to do with the case, the Chileans returned toward the camp with the prisoners. The Chileans in the party drifted away and so when reinforcements came to rescue the Americans, only 11 Chileans remained to become captives of their former prisoners.[17] This incident was expected to be the signal for a general outbreak of trouble between the foreigners and the Americans in the mines, but the Alta California expressed a hope that "the Americans will only visit just punishment on the real offenders."[18] Public opinion soon changed and a public meeting was held in Stockton to uphold the action of the Americans. The meeting expressed the opinion that the Chileans

> had, by false swearing, procured from the Prefect of this place a writ
> for the arrest of Judge Collier and other persons. If this writ had been
> placed in the hands of a proper officer, its injunction would have been
> promptly obeyed. Instead of which it was given to a parcel of the lowest
> order of Chileans--none of whom could speak English--who, instead of
> presenting it in broad day-light, stole upon their unsuspecting victims
> in the dark and dragging them from their beds, tied them; murdering
> all who offered the least resistance. . .[19]

Then followed the inevitable resolution that among other things proclaimed:

> Resolved: That as far as this meeting is informed of the recent
> occurrences in the Calaveras Diggings, the American miners therein
> have acted with a high regard to the good order and welfare of this
> District, and a laudable respect for the rights of themselves and their
> countrymen.[20]

To carry out justice in this case, the Chileans were tried and three of the ringleaders were shot, the rest were flogged and banished from the mines. And as the correspondent of the Alta California reported, "Order is restored--there are no Chileans working on the Mokelumne. . ."[21] That was going to be the basis for establishing order elsewhere in the mines.

An interesting insight into what the Mexican felt in undergoing this persecution is given by an incident told by Coronel in his manuscript Cosas de California. He describes how a party of Americans jumped his claim. The Americans couldn't speak Spanish but their leader made it clear that they claimed the diggings as their own. In writing of it later Coronel recalls

> Excited, I answered him with some harsh words, but fortunately he didn't understand me--in a few moments I could reflect that the value of gold wasn't enough to jeopardize my life in such a manner.[22]

In looking back on these times, the Mexican Californians were unanimous in their explanations for the causes of the trouble. They were that the Sonorans were used to working in mining and consequently found the richest lands and became richer more quickly; that the Mexican Californian--being here on the scene first--was able to take the better lands and was able to learn the mining trade sooner than the Americans; that many of those who came were of criminal or crude social standings;-- and finally, that those who came in 1849 to 1850 were "possessed by the terrible fever to obtain gold. . . they wanted to become rich in a moment."[23]

The Americans gave other reasons for the establishment of their rights and the suppression of the trespassing foreigners on the public domain. These reasons were the ones given in support of a tax on the foreign miners in late 1849 and early 1850. There was no hesitation in making this cause one of national honor and this appeal was painted in glowing words. Bayard Taylor expressed the feeling of the Americans in these words in 1850:[24]

> During the mining season of 1849, more than 15,000 foreigners, mostly Mexicans and Chileans, came in armed bands into the mining districts, bidding defiance to all opposition, and finally carrying out of the country some $20,000,000 worth of gold dust, which belonged by purchase to the people of the United States. If not excluded by law, they will return and recommence the work of plunder. They may, with as much right, gather the harvest in the valley of the Connecticut, the Ohio, or Mississippi.

6

The sinister hand of the foreign capitalist and his agent was detected in this theft of the wealth of California and the national welfare was claimed to be in the balance.

It is a matter of great national policy that the vast amount of California gold, or at least a portion of it, should first find its way through our own country. . . The United States Constitution forbids an export tax; and in the absence of laws in this and other respects, we all know that up to this time three quarters of all the gold sent from this State has passed directly to other nations. The foreign proprietors of gold diggers, and the agents of foreign bankers control at present this matter in their own quiet way . . . . [25]

In the background, too, we can see the beginning of the fear that perhaps the mines were not inexhaustable and that the wealth of the placers would someday run out--perhaps in the near future. An observer in California reflected in summation in his journal on the last day of 1849[26]

The extent of the mineral resources, and more particularly of the gold deposits of California, is still a matter of conjecture; but there is every reason to suppose that the time for accumulating fortunes in a day has nearly gone by; and unless still greater discoveries should be made, at the close of another mining season, with the vast additions which undoubtedly will be made to the numbers of persons operating in the mining districts during the past year, the placeres will be so much exhausted, that they can not be profitably worked without cheap labor and expensive machinery.

The passing of the richest of placers would only mean that the competition would be worse among the miners. As a newspaper in Mexico City observed:

By hard work the strongest and more robust miners earn 16 pesos a day, and many because of bad luck or lack of knowledge in their work, as well as because of physical weakness, waste their time and health in vain searchings. Others more wise have turned to more lucrative work, if they have not returned to that work they practiced before setting out for the gold diggings. [26a]

Within the year the same newspaper would note that competition was so intense in the mines that many Americans were turning to consider filibustering attempts along the Mexican border. [26b]

The preamble to the Foreign Miners' Tax of 1850 is perhaps the clearest and most concise explanation of the reason for the outbreak of feeling against the foreign miner. It pointed out that the mines had brought a multitude of foreigners to California, among whom were a "large portion. . . of desperate characters," that these foreigners took many of the choice locations for mining, that conflicts had broken out to the disturbance of good order and security of the public; and, closing with the ringing proclamation that "it is an inalienable right in the citizens of this State to enjoy and defend life and liberty, to acquire, possess, and protect property, and to pursue and obtain safety and happiness"[27] the new law levied a monthly tax of $20 on any foreigner working in the mines.[28] Such was the beginning of California's first legislated difference between citizen and foreigner in the mines.

The main purpose of the law was to keep out the foreign miner, especially the Hispanic American who had the reputation of being more skillful and lucky at mining.[29] It had the result of keeping out the industrious, sober foreigners, but not the cut-throat, gambler, and thief. It hurt, not the uncommonly skillful or lucky foreigner, but the ordinary plodder who had the same ups and downs as the American miner.[30] Although there was some question in at least a few minds as to the constitutionality as well as the wisdom of this law[31] it went into effect on April 13, 1850.[32]

The agitation caused by this law began even before the law went into effect. In the latter part of May tempers rose in Sonora when the foreigners went to the authorities to complain that the contemplated tax of $20 was beyond reason, but that a tax of three of four dollars would be accepted without any dissatisfaction. The language barrier caused a misunderstanding when one American tried to elbow his way out of the crowd at this meeting, and weapons were drawn. The foreigners left town in alarm. Trouble was complicated when, during the arrest of an armed drunken Mexican, another interfered and was knifed and later died for his troubles.[33] Agitation died out when Americans converged from other camps to help the sheriff, if necessary, collect the tax. Although most the foreigners were hard pressed for money, many of them paid the tax and returned to work. Others left for the mountains, in the hopes of finding new diggings, while many left the mines altogether. One group of five hundred Sonorans left immediately for Mexico.[34] Many of the foreigners declared their intention to become American citizens before the authorities, or claimed citizenship by the right of being in California at the time of the Treaty of Guadalupe. They obtained certificates from the authorities to that effect and used them as protection from abuse in the mines.[35] That the foreigners--especially the Sonorans--were leaving aroused little concern, and no little amusement.

We learn from a private source that in consequence of the probable enforcement of the mining tax the Sonorians are leaving for their own "stomping grounds," in large bodies. We are glad they are taking this step--or these steps rather, but think that they are exhibiting great folly in so doing as so far as their own interests are concerned. "Let 'em go, Johnny."[36]

An inducement to leaving was given by the resolutions of mass meetings which soon sprang up whenever there was any trouble over collecting the tax. For example, a resolution in Sonora passed in July 21, 1850, required all foreigners "not engaged in permanent business and of respectable character" to leave the area within fifteen days, and those who remained had to obtain a permit from a committee and turn over their firearms.[37] So the Sonorans left, and in such numbers that the law was soon repealed for fundamental economic reasons.

By September, 1850, from one half to three quarters of the Mexicans had left the Southern mining area.[38] The exodus caused by the tax, aggravated by an extremely dry winter,[39] ruined some of the southern mining camps. Columbia was reduced to only nine or ten men during this winter.[40] The Mexicans had been estimated at about 15,000 in number in the southern mines,[41] with about 10,000 of them in the Sonora region alone,[42] so the effects of the loss of this market on the merchants of California can be estimated. When it was realized that the loss of business could be in large part attributed to this law, the businessmen and the press began to clamor for its repeal. One by one the reasons for its passage were attacked.

> Much has been said of the amounts of gold taken from the mines by Sonorans, Chileans and Peruvians, and taken out of the country. As a general fact. . . not one pound in ten, gathered by these foreigners, is shipped off to their credit: it is spent in the country for provisions, clothing and in the hazards of the gaming table.[43]

The Alta California on March 7, 1851, after beginning its editorial with a review of the past American policy of open migration and freedom of economic equality said:

> Knowing this, tens of thousands of miners came to California. . . . From Mexico and Peru and Chile they flocked here, better miners than our own people to work and to purchase, and they furnished the supply. They usually expended nearly all of their gold as they lived. . . . Even those who occasionally left for their homes, generally purchases a good stock of various articles before leaving. . . . Our own countrymen came here only to make a pile and carry it out of the country. They seldom purchased anything to take away, and expended just as little as possible in the country while they remained here.[44]

Lynch law or even secession from the state was hinted if the bill would not be repealed;[45] resolutions were passed that, as always, expressed great feeling.

Resolved, That we look upon the infliction of this tax upon the people of the southern district, as but part of a grand scheme to depress the enterprise of our citizens. . . to cripple our commerce and destroy our local trade.

Resolved, That said law, notwithstanding the decision of the Supreme Court of this State, is unconstitutional, and has been so declared by every sound lawyer in the Union who has been consulted thereupon.

Resolved, That the infliction of this tax upon our district is unconstitutional, unlawful, an outrage upon the particular miner, and of vast injury to the whole population of this district, and as a public measure, its continuance under existing United States and State laws, is a public robbery.[46]

The repeal of the law was signed on March 14, 1851. The Alta California could not resist the temptation to orate on its demise, so the law passed into history speeded by these words:

Let our Chilean friends and Mexican neighbors, the Gaul and the Briton, the Celestial and the Kanaka, hombres from the land of Pizarro and Mynheers from submarine Holland, let them all come and work with us, and become part of us, full of confidence that justice and policy will never again be so outraged as in that unfortunate law whose death writ the Governor has proclaimed.[47]

This complete reversal of policy was aided by the change that was taking place in the mines. By the end of 1850, the southern mines were well worked over and already there were quartz mines to a depth of fifty feet.[48] All through the spring of 1851 the talk in the newspapers was about quartz mining and little on placers.[49] When as an April Fools Day joke an ad was placed in the Alta California for men to work in the mines for wages of ten dollars a day, over a hundred men plagued the Mexican couple whose address had been given.[50] By the summer, wages were $20 to $30 a week and board, although most miners went prospecting as soon as they saved a "grubstake."[51] By this time, it was admitted that the age of the placer mine was over and quartz mining was the new industry.[52]

The need grew up for a new kind of miner, one who would work for wages. The American would rather "work on his own hook" and would rather take a chance on becoming the owner of a rich mine, so the burden of working the southern mines fell to the Mexican and Chilean.[53] A portion of them had stayed on stubbornly through all the trouble around Sonora[54] and when the first rash of troubles were over in September,

1850, they were being joined by compatriots at the rate of forty to fifty a day.[55]
Large numbers of Peruvians came to California in 1851 and early 1852 because of
the internal troubles and revolution in Peru.[56] These miners were welcomed now,
for

> During the winter. . . business was dull. . . but the sun shone behind
> the cloud and is now breaking over our land. . . The accessions. . .
> to our population are of daily occurrence. . . and within one month
> past, 10,000 Mexicans have arrived in the Mariposa and Tuolomne
> regions have become customers.[57]

The troubles after this period, until the outbreak suddenly of anti-Chinese
feelings, were of one kind: the result of attempts to take from foreign miners rich
mining claims that they had discovered and developed.[58] Even then they made it clear
that they had nothing against the foreigner working for wages.[59] One method that was
used to attempt to circumvent the bias against a Spaniard or Mexican owning a quartz
claim was to form a company in which the Hispanic discoverors would take in Americans as partners.[60] Gradually the idea developed that claims should be held by
American citizens or those who had declared their intention to become citizens.[61]

The development of the prejudice against the Chinese in the mines is incidental to the story of the Mexicans in that industry, because the prejudice grew and
was transferred from just the Chinese to all foreign labor. It is interesting to note
that it shows, however, the difference between the economic interests of the merchants and businessmen of California and the economic interests of the miners that
had laready grown up. When the Chinese first came to California, they were praised
for ability to adapt themselves to American society and their value to California in
general.

> They are among the most industrious, quiet, patient people among us.
> Perhaps citizens of no nation except the Germans, are more quiet and
> valuable. They seem to live under our laws as if born and bred under
> them, and already have commenced an expression of their preference
> by applying for citizenship. . . .[62]

When, in late 1851, a group of Chinese were expelled from the Yuba River, after
building a dam to divert the river on the claim they had purchased, other Americans
helped to reestablish them on their claim.[63]

Yet in the spring of 1852 feeling grew so quickly against them that it resulted
in the passage of the second Foreign Miners Tax. The reasons for this sudden emergence

of feeling can be found partly in the vast numbers of them that came suddenly in 1852, but primarily in the fact that they were being hired in China on contracts that gave them from \$3 to \$4 a month and board.[64]

Surprisingly enough it was not the miners who first complained about the contract labor in California, but the contractors. They found it impossible to enforce the contracts here and wanted a law to make them binding in California.[65] The law was almost passed, but when miners began to think about what it meant to them, they began to talk, hold meetings, and pass resolutions against the Chinese. The miner realized the allies that the Chinese had, for in a resolution passed in Columbia on May 8, 1852, they condemned the ship owners, capitalists and merchants who wanted to flood the state with cheap labor in order to sell more goods.[66] Commercial interests, however, still held that the Chinese

> . . . contribute in no small degree to the general prosperity by consuming food, clothing, and impliments of labor, by giving employment to ocean and inland shipping, and by the general addition in a hundred ways to the business of the country.[67]

In the resolutions and meetings that were held during the month of May, 1852, the complaints gradually changed from against the Chinese to foreign miners in general.[68] When the second Foreign Miners tax went into effect on the first of June, 1852, the provisions called for a monthly tax of \$3 for every foreign miner in the gold fields.[69] This was raised to \$4 in 1853.[70] There was little trouble in collecting the tax from the foreign miners[71] but the miners often ignored paying it when not pressed by collectors for it. Some Americans used the lack of payment as an excuse to jump the claims of foreigners.[72] When they did, troubles broke out again. At Mariposita, on the Mariposa River, in late June, some Americans ousted the foreigners because they had not payed their taxes. The fact that they could not pay it as there was no collector appointed for the area, didn't seem to bother the Americans who ordered all the foreigners to leave the mines within twenty-four hours.[73] But by the ninth of the next month, the French consul was in Mariposa to help straighten out the affairs of French citizens. First the French and then the Mexicans had their claims restored.[74] This restoration more than anything else showed how much had changed in the mines.

The difference in the opinions of the miners and the merchants can also be seen in the reception in San Francisco to the results of the miners conventions held in 1852. When a resolution in Sacramento called for "a difference in the privilege extended to miners who are citizens of foreign countries and those who are citizens of this,"[75] the press could point out that "It being evident that unworthy motives are mixed up with their views, very little confidence is placed in their deliberations."[76] The Assemblies and Resolutions could be appraised at the time in these words:

> The resolutions and expressions of opinion of the various conventions of miners are so dissimilar, so unreconcilable, and so partial in their character. . . .

> All the schemes proposed are merely local in their character, and appear more intended to protect the separate interests of some particular and individual company, than to evince a desire to advance the interests of all. . . .[77]

During 1853 the feeling developed that the Miners Tax was insufficient to protect the interests of the American miner. The feeling that the payment of a "paltry tax" gave the foreigner the rights of citizenship with none of the duties and responsibilities.[78] The resolution excluding the non-citizen or one who had not declared intentions of becoming a citizen were used more and more to exclude the Chinese.[79] The troubles with the Mexicans seemed to be caused in 1853 by emotions aroused by the exploits of notorious Mexican bandit Joaquin who terrorized the southern mines.[80] By the end of 1853 and early 1854, the Miners Tax was used only against the Chinese and discrimination was limited mainly to that group.[81]

Looking back on this six year period, with the unsettled position of the Mexican miner in the gold fields, we can trace some of his attempts to find and establish a stable economic position. As has already been noted, many solved the problem by leaving the mines, either returning to their foreign homes or to their ranches in California. Others stayed in the mines turning to less attractive phases of mining when discrimination broke out. The Mexicans were the first to go into quartz mining; the American miner only thought of quartz mining when the river or gulch placers were worked out.[82] The quartz mines were generally unsuccessful until the development of new mining processes in the Comstock Lode made the gold mines in California practical on a working basis. The only successful quartz miners as a class were the Mexicans. Experienced in quartz mining, they were willing to take the special pains which made mining too slow for most Americans.[83] They used the arrastra, and worked only the richest pieces of ore. Profits came slowly, but as J. Ross Browne observed fiftenn years later

With experience in the observation of quartz, and a mode of working in which failure was almost impossible, these Mexicans frequently did very well.[84]

This experience, both from Mexico and from California, made Mexican miners welcome at first in the Comstock mines.[85] Many processes used and introduced by the Mexicans were the basis for American improvements; for example, the patio process and crude working of tailings were refined by the ingenuity of the Americans.[86] These improvements were of such an extent that the Mexican obtained the reputation of being old fashioned and primitive in later years.[87]

The Mexicans also escaped the persecution by working for an American, either for wages or shared of the profits.[88] The Mexicans all through this period escaped from persecution or violence whenever they could find an American they knew to vouch for them.[89] When, in later years, more and more miners were working for wages, the Mexicans and foreigners tended to do the plain manual labor tasks while the Americans became specialists in handling equipment and machinery.[90]

Another field of mining which the Mexicans and Chileans soon moved to was the working of the quicksilver mines, especially at New Almaden.[91] As early as September, 1849, the New Almaden, advertised in Spanish in the Alta California for employees among "Hispanic-Americans of good conduct." This was one of the first advertisements in California that offered employment.[92] By 1851 the mine was in full operation, employing some two hundred laborers in that mine alone.[93] Miners contracted to remove the ore, the price given depending on the ease with which the ore could be extracted. In later years, when a large number of Cornishmen also worked in the quicksilver mines, the Mexicans were noted for willingness to undertake jobs which the Cornishmen had abandoned.[94]

An allied field that the Mexicans soon took to was that of freight hauling. Some of the early California rancheros, when they arrived in the mines in 1849, came with large amounts of provisions. When they saw the high prices which could be obtained for the fruits of their ranchos, some gave up mining and turned to the business of supplying the miners with the necessities of life.[95] When the Americans saw the profits that were being made, they too turned to freight business. Whenever troubles against the foreigners in the mines broke out the Mexican trader was sure to lose his stock and investment, because the Americans were quick to take advantage of the position that the Mexican would be placed.[96] Up until 1850, most

14

of the owners and operators of mule freight lines were Mexicans, but with the increased numbers of Americans coming to the mines, some American bought up mule teams, and hired Mexicans to work for them. [97] The majority of the mule drivers always remained Mexican, because of the skill involved in loading the mules, although control of the freighting business passed into the hands of Americans. [98] As an English traveler observed:

> A month's daily practice is unsufficient to make an apt scholar a moderately good packer. One may watch the mode of fastening the load with a riata for a year twice a day and be no more able to do it at a twelve months end than the flute could be learned by looking at another blow and finger it. [99]

The American attitude toward this group varied as the economic value of the Mexicans to the American society varied. The areas of acceptance changed as conditions in California changed, but the basic concept of the position of the Mexican remained the same. To the majority of Americans, whether they expressed it openly or merely implied it by their actions, the position of the Mexicans was decided early in this period.

> When gold shall begin to fail, or require capital or machinery, you will want these hardy men to quarry the rocks and feed your stampers, and when you shall plunge into the Cinnebar mountains, you will want them to sink your shafts and kindle fires under your quicksilver retorts. They will become the hewers of wood and the drawers of water to American capital and enterprise. But if you want to perform this drugery yourself, drive out the Sonorians, and upset that cherished system of political economy founded in a spirit of wisdom and national justice. [100]

[1]George Hyde, <u>Statement of Historical Facts on California</u> (Unpublished Manuscript in Bancroft Library, Berkeley, California), first draft, p. 26.

[2]Robert Glass Cleland, <u>A History of California: The American Period</u> (New York: Macmillan Co., 1928), pp. 280-281.

[3]John Walton Caughey, <u>Gold is the Cornerstone</u> (Berkeley and Los Angeles, 1938), p. 195; and Josiah Royce, <u>California</u> (New York: Knopf, 1938), pp. 286-287.

[4]Antonio Franco Coronel, <u>Cosas de California</u> (Unpublished Manuscript in Bancroft Library, Berkeley, California), p. 178; and Bayard Taylor, <u>El Dorado, or Adventures in the Path of Empire</u> (New York: Knopf, 1949), p. 69.

[5]John S. Hittell, <u>Mining in the Pacific States of North America</u> (San Francisco, 1861), p. 15; William Kelly, <u>A Stroll Through the Diggings of California</u> (Oakland: Biobooks, 1950), p. 13; and Rodman Paul, <u>California Gold</u> (Cambridge, Mass.: Harvard University Press, 1947), p. 112.

[6]J. Tywhitt Brooks, <u>Four Months Among the Gold Finders in Alta California</u> (New York: D. Appleton & Co., 1849), pp. 21-39; Coronel, op. cit., pp. 141-142; Augustine Janssens, <u>Vida y Aventuras en California</u> (Unpublished Manuscript in Bancroft Library, Berkeley, Calif.), p. 198; and J. J. Pico, <u>Acontesimientos</u> (Unpublished Manuscript in Bancroft Library, Berkeley, Calif.), p. 77.

[7]Janssens, op. cit., pp. 199-206. (The translation is mine.)

[8]Marrano G. Vallejo, <u>Documentos para la Historia de California, 1769-1850</u> (Unpublished Manuscripts in Bancroft Library, Berkeley, Calif.) Vol. 13, document 15.

[9]Ibid., document 48.

[10]Pico, op. cit., p. 77.

[11]Kelly, op. cit., pp. 15-16.

[12]Coronel, op. cit., p. 166. (The translation is mine.)

[13]Enos Christman, <u>One Man's Gold</u> (New York: McGraw-Hill, 1930), pp. 171-172.

[14]San Francisco <u>Alta California,</u> August 2, 1849.

[15]Ibid., September 18, 1849.

[16]Ibid., October 25, 1849.

[17]Robert Wilson in a letter from Stockton, California, December 31, 1849, in <u>Alta California,</u> January 5, 1850.

[18] _Alta California_, January 5, 1850.

[19] Robert Wilson in a letter from Stockton, California, January 3, 1850, in _Alta California_, January 5, 1850.

[20] Ibid., (Italics are mine).

[21] Robert Wilson in a letter from Stockton, California, February 3, 1850, in _Alta California_, February 9, 1850.

[22] Coronel, op. cit., p. 166 (The translation is mine).

[23] Coronel, op. cit., p. 182 (The translation is mine).

[24] Taylor, op. cit., p. 372.

[25] _Journal of the Senate of the State of California_, 1850, pp. 493-497.

[26] Albert Lyman, _Journal of a Voyage to California and Life in the Gold Diggings_ (New York: 1852), p. 146.

[26a] _El Siglo XIX_, January 16, 1850. (The translation is mine.)

[26b] Ibid., January 27, 1851.

[27] As quoted in _Alta California_, April 22, 1850.

[28] _Statutes of California passed at the First Session of Legislature, 1849-1850_, p. 221.

[29] Hubert Howe Bancroft, _History of California_ (San Francisco, 1884-1890), vol. VI, p. 388: and Royce, op. cit., p. 282.

[30] Royce, Ibid., p. 284.

[31] _Alta California_, April 22, 1850.

[32] Royce, Ibid., p. 284.

[33] Robert Wilson in letters from Sonora, Calif., May 19 to 22, 1850, in the _Alta California_, May 27, 1850.

[34] Ibid., May 31, 1850, in _Alta California_, June 3, 1850.

[35] _Alta California_, July 1, 1850 (Stepmer Edition) and 31st Congress, 1st Session, H. Ex. Doc. 17, pp. 698 & 700.

[36] _Alta California_, May 24, 1850.

[37] Theodore Henry Hittell, History of California (San Francisco, 1885-89), vol. III, p. 709.

[38] J. Heckendon and W. A. Wilson, Miners' and Business Mens' Directory (Columbia, 1856), p. 183.

[39] Alta California, February 7, February 8, and February 21, 1850.

[40] Herbert O. Lang, A History of Tuolomne County, California (San Francisco, 1882), pp. 26-28.

[41] Hittell, op. cit., p. 706.

[42] Report of T. Butler King, March 22, 1850, in Taylor, op. cit., p. 365.

[43] Walter Colton, Three Years in California (New York, 1850), p. 367.

[44] Alta California, March 17, 1851.

[45] William Hooper in a letter from Stockton, California, March 5, 1851, in the Alta California, March 7, 1851.

[46] Resolution in Stockton, California, March 6, 1851, as reported in Alta California, March 10, 1851.

[47] Alta California, March 20, 1851.

[48] Ibid., November 2, 1850.

[49] See for example Alta California, March 3, 1851.

[50] Ibid., April 3, 1851.

[51] Ibid., July 30, 1851.

[52] Ibid., July 17, 1851.

[53] Stockton (Calif.,) Journal, September 19, 1851.

[54] Paul, op. cit., p. 111.

[55] Alta California, September 2, 1850.

[56] Ibid., April 5, 1852.

[57] Ibid., April 21, 1851 (the italics are mine).

[58] Royce op. cit., pp. 287-288; Thomas Allsop, California and its Gold Mines (London, 1855), p. 25; Alta California for July 11, November 27 and 28, 1851, January 4 and March 22, 1852; Stockton Journal, April 28, 1851. Some word should

be made on two incidents which occurred in mid-1852 which do not seem to agree with this statement. The first is the lynching of the Mexican woman Juanita in Downieville (see Caughey, op. cit., pp. 188, 236; and Royce, op. cit., pp. 290-295 for treatments of this event) and the branding of a horsethief and flogging of a gold dust counterfeiter at Sonora (see Alta California, July 11, 1852), both of which occurred on the 5th of July 1852. A possible explanation is that much excitement and feeling was aroused by the Vigilance Committees in San Francisco, Sacramento, Stockton, Sonora and Downieville at this time and the remaining effects of the excess of patriotic and alcoholic spirits from the fourth of July celebrations of the day before clouded the good judgment of the Americans involved.

[59] Alta California, July 11, 1851.

[60] Alta California, August 1 and October 20, 1851, March 1, 1853.

[61] Resolution at Sonora, California, October 12, 1852, in Alta California, October 18, 1852; Convention at Jamestown, California, September 18, 1852, in Alta California, September 28, 1852.

[62] Alta California, May 12, 1851.

[63] Ibid., October 11, 1851.

[64] Journal of the Senate of the Legislature of the State of California, 1852, pp. 373-378.

[65] Alta California, March 8, 1852.

[66] Ibid., May 15, 1852.

[67] Ibid., April 26, 1852.

[68] Ibid., May 3, 5, 14, and 22, 1852.

[69] Bancroft, op. cit., p. 406.

[70] The Statutes of California Passed at the Session of Legislature, 1853, pp. 62-65.

[71] Alta California, June 15, 1852.

[72] Ibid., August 3, 1852.

[73] Ibid., July 1, 1852.

[74] Ibid., July 15, 1852.

[75] Ibid., January 24, 1852.

[76] Ibid., February 1, 1852.

[77] Ibid., August 5, 1851.

[78] Ibid., January 24, February 7, February 15, and June 29, 1853.

[79] J. Ross Browne, Report on the Mineral Resources of the United States (Washington, 1867), pp. 236, 238 and 240; Heckendon and Wilson, op. cit., p. 8.

[80] Alta California, January 29, 1853.

[81] E. S. Capron, History of California (Boston, 1854), pp. 235, 236.

[82] Allsop, op. cit., p. 35.

[83] J. Ross Browne, Report on the Mineral Resources of the United States (Washington, 1868), p. 8.

[84] Browne, Report, 1867, p. 21.

[85] Dan DeQuille (William Wright), The Big Bonanza (New York, 1947), p. 86; and Charles Howard Shinn, The Story of the Mine (New York, 1903), pp. 79-80.

[86] DeQuille, op. cit., p. 260 and Shinn, op. cit., pp. 87-88.

[87] J. D. Borthwick, Three years in California (London, 1851), p. 31.

[88] Taylor, op. cit., p. 66; Alta California, October 25, 1849; and Jessie Benton Fremont and Francis Preston Fremont, Great Events during the life of Major General Fremont and of Jessie Benton Fremont (Unpublished manuscript at Bancroft Library, Berkeley, California), p. 99.

[89] Coronel, op. cit., pp. 159-160; Janssens, op. cit., pp. 203-204; and Alta California, July 1, 1852.

[90] Paul, op. cit., p. 323.

[91] William Henry Brewer, Up and Down California in 1860-64 (New Haven and London, 1931), pp. 139-140.

[92] Alta California, September 27, 1849. See also issues from October 11 to November 22, 1849.

[93] Ibid., October 19, 1851.

[94] Browne, Report, 1867, p. 172.

[95] Jose M. Amador, Memorias Sobre la Historia de California (Unpublished manuscript in the Bancroft Library, Berkeley, California), pp. 177-184; Coronel, op. cit., pp. 170-172.

[96] Ibid.

97 Edward W. McIlhany, _Recollection of a '49er_ (Kansas City, Mo., 1908), pp. 56-64.

98 Taylor, op. cit., p. 75.

99 John Keats Lord, _The Naturalist in Vancouver Island and British Columbia_ (London, 1866), p. 208, as found in Joseph McGowan, _Freighting in the Mines in California, 1849-1859_ (Unpublished Ph.D. Thesis, University of California, Berkeley, California), p. 180.

100 Colton, op. cit., p. 368.

CHAPTER II

THE FRUITS OF THE LAND:

THE DECLINE OF THE MEXICAN AMERICAN LAND HOLDER

IN CALIFORNIA, 1846-1875

The military commanders of the United States forces during the conquest of
California had assured the Mexican-Californians that they would not be disturbed in
their rights as property owners by the change in governments. The Treaty of Guadalupe Hidalgo in its Ninth Article assured the Californians that they would "be maintained and protected in the free enjoyment of their liberty and property, and secured
in the free exercise of their religion without restriction." General Bennet Riley, in
assuming the position of ex-officio head of the civil government of California in 1849
stressed that he was doing so under the laws of the ex-Mexican possession, and
pointed out that

> The military government ended with the war, and what remains is
> the civil government recognized in the existing laws of California. . . .
> The laws of California not inconsistent with the laws, constitution
> and treaties of the United States are still in force, and must continue
> in force until changed by competent authority.[1]

The Californians felt that the United States government was clearly obligated
to confirm the land grants that had been issued by the Spanish and Mexican governments.
Their struggle to keep these lands, which in many cases had been in the family for a
generation, was a major phase in their adaptation to the new American society which
had come to the Pacific coast of North America.

The ultimate loss of these lands can be traced to a combination of political,
economic, and social causes whose cumulative effect was such that the keeping by any
Mexican-American of a large part of rancho land could be only a remote possibility.

The first major blow to the owners of the ranchos was the passage of the
Land Act in 1851. The law, as administered in California, while technically within
the letter of the obligations of the United States, violated the spirit of all the guarantees
given the Mexican Californians and insured that the majority of the lands granted would
be stripped from the grantees. The reasons for the ultimate policy were threefold:
the American misunderstanding of the nature and economic foundation for the large

grants; the growing demand for a national "free-land" policy which was to culmin-
ate in the Homestead Act of 1862; and the racial prejudice of many of the newcomers to California.

The American settlers in California did not understand the need for the
large areas of land granted to the Californians. Used to more intensive forms of
agricultural pursuits, the practice of grazing large numbers of cattle untended on
vast acres of lands seemed both extravagant and indolent. During the period of the
grants, land was abundant and it took several acres to support one cow; consequently
holdings of up to 50,000 acres were not excessive. Until the gold rush, cattle were
raised primarily for their value in supplying hides and tallow; consequently, it was
possible to own thousands of acres of land and many head of cattle and still not be
rich.[2]

The Californians were also struggling against the growing demands for free
public land. Since as early as 1820 it had been possible to purchase land from the
public domain for as little as $1.25 an acre. In 1846 the first Homestead Act was
presented in Congress; its provisions were to give land from the public domain to
those who would settle and improve it. Only the sectional rivalries of the day
delayed passage of a Homestead Act until 1862.[3] The feelings of the land-hungry
Americans upon their arrival in California can be well imagined when they discovered that "most of the good grazing land along the coast and coastal rivers, along
with a part of the San Joaquin and Sacramento valleys, was privately owned rancho
land--land. . . the gift of the government to individual Mexican citizens."[4] There
can be little doubt that Congress was informed on these feelings.

The problem of the land grants was also complicated by the racial feelings
of the time. The Americans flooding California were children of the age of Mani-
fest Destiny and felt that "the great landowners were merely monopolists who,
like the Indians, were obstructing the path of progress of civilization."[5] The feeling
of the Anglo-Saxon newcomer was simple in regard to the native Californians: "The
Mexicans were descendants of the Spanish; the Spanish had Moorish blood; ergo, the
Mexicans were Hottentots at the very least."[6]

The Mexican Californians had support from many open-minded Americans.
Senator Thomas Hart Benton, of Missouri, fought for a simple plan of confirmation
for the land grants, pointing out that prolonging the litigation was in effect equal to

confiscation.[7] A contemporary visitor to California summed up the defense of the Mexican Californians and gave a plea for quick and liberal settlement of the land claims in these words:[8]

> . . . few of them have _all_ the forms prescribed by legislative enact-
> ments, but they have official insignia to certify the intentions of the
> (Mexican) government. To disturb grants would be alike impolitic
> and unjust; it would convert the lands which they cover to the public
> domain, and ultimately turn them over to speculators and foreign
> capitalists. Better let them remain where they are; they are in good
> hands; they are held mostly by Californians--a class of persons who
> part with them on reasonable terms. No Californian grinds the face
> of the poor, or refuses an emigrant participation in his lands. I have
> seen them dispose of miles for a consideration less than would be
> required by Americans for as many acres. You are shut up to the
> shrewdness of the Yankee on the one hand, and the liberality of the
> Californian on the other.

The Land Act of 1851 had its supporters who insisted that the law was entirely just and that all the rights of the grantees were and would continue to be respected. Senator William N. Gwin of California, the law's proponent, posed the question on the Senate floor.

> Can any honest board of commissioners fail to decide in favor of
> any bona fide claim, where the claimant has complied with the law,
> or where, under the custom and usages of the Spanish and Mexican
> Governments, they would have been confirmed, although all the re-
> quirements of the law were not fully met? And will not such a decision
> be affirmed by the Supreme Court of the United States?[9]

A look at the judgments of the courts requires a positive answer to this question. A tendency to refuse grants on technicalities in some cases worked apparent injustices. The case which seemingly has the least justification in its final verdict was the New Almaden case. The quicksilver mine had passed to the control of a British company, and its mineral claim was rejected by the Supreme Court of the United States on apparently reasons of national interest.[10]

The main complaint against the Land Law was not that the Commission or Courts were unfair or unjust, however; the most that could be said of them is that they did not understand the Mexican land systems or local conditions, and that they often were too legalistic. The most obnoxious feature of the law was to place the burden of proof on the land owner. The importance placed by the Commission and the Court on documents and their strict interpretation on the legal, rather than the moral bases for the claims, made the approval of the land grants a long and expensive process. This, rather than any injustice on the part of the commissioners or judges, was the main complaint.

The inability of many of the grantees to produce documents to prove their claims led to expensive deputations from witnesses who knew of the granting of the land and to lengthy searches into the archives for corroborating papers. The prior governments of California had not been systematic or complete in its paperwork; but the law, rather than taking this into consideration, insisted on setting up criteria more compatible to the American system of land titles than to the Mexican which they were to judge. The defenders of the Land Act of 1851 blame most of the troubles on the lack of system in the records of the land grants and not on the means of proving them insisted upon by the American authorities. An example of setting the American land system and title practice as the yardstick rather than the Mexican can be found in the comments of a prominent member of the California legal profession:

> The fundamental error was with the Mexican territorial authorities who failed to give to their grantees proper evidence of the titles to the lands granted. . .

> Another serious fault on the part of the Mexican authorities was their neglect and lack of system in preserving and recording the evidence of titles in their archives. . . With such a system (as used by the Americans), the Spanish and Mexican land claims referred to in the treaty could have been disposed of by the courts in less than two years.[11]

The chronic dearth of capital and ready money in California made the expenses of a long litigation difficult to meet. Until the grant was approved the grant lands were not salable,[12] and many of the rancheros had to resort to borrowing money at ruinous rates of interest in order to prosecute their claims. Interest rates of five to eight percent compounded monthly were common; while for a small amount a rate of twelve and one half per cent compounded daily was not unheard of.[13] An idea of what these rates meant can be better understood when it is realized that at the rate of eight per cent compounded monthly, the principal is doubled in a little over nine months.

All these factors working together--the necessity of proving their grants under a legal system with which they were unfamiliar, the heavy expense of long and extended litigation, and the necessity of borrowing money at usurous rates--took a heavy toll of the Californian land grant holders. In Los Angeles County it has been estimated that one out of ten grant holders was pushed into bankruptcy by the expenses of trying to prove his claims and that two fifths of the land was disposed of in order to finance the claims of the grantees.[14]

The Commission and the Courts did confirm a majority of the grants presented to it, and most of the grantees had their lands and titles cleared, even if the process was long and expensive. The Land Act of 1851 was not the only factor in stripping the land from the Mexican Californians. The process had begun as soon as the first foreigner had set foot in California. They observed that by hard work a large land estate could be built. Some of them purchased lands from the original grantee; some became Mexican citizens and received land grants from the government themselves. By the time of the Land Commission, only a small majority of the claims approved went to Mexican Californians. A breakdown of the figures gives an idea of how much of the land had already passed from their control. Of the 813 cases presented to the Commission, 521 were confirmed by the time the Commission adjourned in 1856;[15] this number was raised to 604 by successful appeals to the courts.[16] Of these 604 cases only 330 were confirmed to Californians of Mexican descent.[17]

The Mexican Californians were given approved titles to over five million acres of land; and they controlled at least temporarily most of the best land of the state.[18] Yet it has been estimated that by 1891 there were not more than thirty Mexican Americans who had retained any measure of the prestige that this economic advantage should have given them.[19] A comprehensive story of the land passing from their hands is yet to be written; the best work to date is limited to southern California with the emphasis on Los Angeles County. Although some of the generalizations and conclusions are not valid for the entire state, the reasons for the breakup of the land holdings in southern California show some indication of what happened all over California.

> During the period (1850 to 1866) . . . most of the great land holdings in Southern California passed from the hands of native Californians into the hands of Americans. . . . It was brought about by the Land Act of 1851. . .; by the prodigality, extravagance and financial ineptitude of the native Californians; by inequitable short-term mortgages and fantastically high interest rates; by a prolonged depression in the cattle industry, following a period of

sky-rocketing prices produced by the Gold Rush; and finally by the historic drought of the mid-sixties, which caused a widespread revolution in the life and customs of Southern California.[20]

Other factors that speeded the passing of the large land holding in California were the lack of ready capital to expand agricultural pursuits, an unfavorable state government, and social customs. The Mexican Californians, who failed to understand the value of a signed document in the American legal system, were capitalized upon by sharp Yankee newcomers. They were prevailed upon to sign papers they did not understand.[21] Rancho San Barnabe in the Salinas Valley was sold during the drought of 1863-64 for $500 when the owner thought he was signing a bill of sale for ten times that amount.[22] Jose Domingo Peralta, whose confirmed title to three different grants would give the impression that he at least could hold his own in the new society, signed a mortgage thinking he was leasing the property.[23]

Some of the land holders seemed to be trying their best to lose their lands. Guillermo Castro was given a confirmed land grant title to the 26,000 acres of Rancho San Lorenzo in Alameda county by the 285th claim presented to the Land Commission.[24] Close enough to San Francisco to have a ready market for its products, yet far enough away so not to be threatened with immediate influx of Americans, it would seem that Castro was in a position to do extremely well. Yet he quickly lost his land in a series of ill-timed steps.

> Castro's first bad move. . . was made in 1852, when he took $35,000 with him to the southern country to buy stock. . . . He could not keep the money until he made the purchase, and he spent it in gambling. In 1856 he mortgaged his ranch. Then he sold enough land. . . to get out of debt, besides $8,000 to $10,000 which he unprofitably spent in San Francisco. It was then that he had to mortgage to (Faxton D.) Atherton (of Menlo Park). . .

In 1864 title to Rancho San Lorenzo passed to Atherton for the added consideration of $30,000.[25]

The second generation seemed to be doing its best to lose the lands also. Instead of presenting a common front in order to protect their common interests, many fought among themselves. Appeals to the courts often brought redistribution of the estate, but the major portion usually went for court and lawyer fees. Such a fight occurred among the Castro family over the division of the San Pablo Rancho in Contra Costa county and was one of the main reasons for the land passing from their hands.[26] The legal battles lasted for over forty years and the final settlement fees alone in 1894 were over $103,000.[27] A similar quarrel over Rancho Canada del Hambre in Contra Costa County similarly enriched the growing legal profession of California.[28] It was inevitable that some of the second generation would prefer the activities of the towns rather than the life on the ranchos. Although such a practice could never lead to the increase of their holdings and indeed could never lead to their loss, the heirs of Feliciano Soberanes by 1862 found it more to their liking to lease the Rancho San Lorenzo in Monterey county and spend their time in Monterey.[29]

The usurious rates of interest have already been alluded to, but a few examples will serve to show that only a small amount needed to serve as the seed of destruction of a large land holding. Manuel Garfias' claim to Rancho San Pasqual in Los Angeles county was approved by the Land Commission and the District Court for 13,693.93 acres. But before the patent to the land was issued in 1863 the land had passed from his hands. Garfias' attempt to make a good impression in the new American society in California caused his downfall. He built a house for $5000 on borrowed money. The fact that the house was well known for its comfort and style did not decrease the ruinous interest rates. While he was treasurer of Los Angeles in 1850 to 1851 he left the ranch under the control of his mother-in-law. He was forced to deed the ranch to Benjamin D. Wilson in January of 1859 for a disclosed consideration of $1800.[30] The compound interest rates multiplied the amounts borrowed at a rapid rate, and the common practice was to pay off a small note and its accumulated interest with a larger note. In 1861 Julio Verdugo borrowed on his land and signed a note for $3,445.37 at an interest of three percent per month. In eight years this had grown to $58,750 and Verdugo lost the part of the San Rafael rancho that he had inherited.[31] Horace Bell tells the story of a rapidly growing debt of Jose del Carmen Lugo. Lugo signed a note for $2720 to settle previous small loans. The note was signed on June 9, 1854, and drew five percent interest per month, compounded monthly. At this rate it grew to $13,127.54 when a judgment was given for that amount by the District Court, the judgment to carry the same interest as the original note.[32] The holder of this note is identified by Bell as a governor of the state; an Irishman who came to the state in 1851, married a Mexican girl, and built up a fortune of over two million dollars--mainly from the profits of judicious loans--from the five hundred dollar dowry his wife brought him.[33] But perhaps the ultimate refinement in the loan business in California was attained by David Jacks in the Salinas Valley. He paid the delinquent taxes without notifying the owners; when this was brought to the owners' attention, he generously offered to relinquish his claim on their property if they would pay him back his money with interest. By taking advantage of the Mexicans lack of attention to tax matters, Jacks had found a way to force loans upon the Mexican land holders.[34]

The years 1863 and 1864 were ones of drought unequaled in the memory of the white man in California. Cleland shows a graphic picture of the effects of these years on southern California and concludes that they were the death blow to the ranchero and his way of life.

> . . . (A) few Spanish Californians. . . had been able to maintain
> at least a portion of their original holdings until the coming of the
> drought. Almost none, even of that small number, survived the
> widespread ruin of the mid-sixties. Reduced by mounting debts
> and unpaid taxes. . . the little that was left of their once lordy
> estates passed forever into alien hands. . . . The day of unfenced
> ranchos, of enormous herds of half-wild cattle, of manorial estates,
> and pleasure-loving paisanos came to its inevitable close.[35]

The effects of the drought were especially hard on Los Angeles county. In 1864 five sixths of the tax payers of the county were delinquent.[36] The effects of the drought in other parts of the state, while still great, were mitigated by other factors.

In Monterey county the drought was severe during these two years; one ranchero alone estimated that his losses in these two years were from $300,000 to $400,000. Yet this same ranchero was able to make enough money in 1865 to pay off a $22,000 debt.[37] Those ranchos on the coast in Monterey had a slight advantage for the fogs provided some moisture. Although the rancheros had to sell great parts of their land and mortgage heavily in order to buy feed, some weathered the crisis with at least part of their holdings.[38]

In present-day Ventura county, although the area suffered heavily from the drought and the flood of 1861-62 which preceeded it, the rancheros gradually recovered. The ranchos here were not as heavily overstocked as those in Los Angeles and were in a better position to come through the crisis. The drought was not the main cause for the breakup of the ranchos in this area, but rather the large flood of immigration to the area from 1863 on.[39]

San Diego county had suffered from the effects of a flood in the years 1861-

1862 and it suffered severely from the effects of the drought in the following two years. The disaster, however, was not as severe in San Diego for two reasons. The ranchos of the county were not as heavily stocked as those to the north; more important, there was more unclaimed mountain range that could be used until the coast feed improved. These two factors mitigated the effects of the drought on breaking up the ranchos in the county.[40]

One of the difficulties facing the large land holders who were trying to maintain their position was the lack of governmental support for their interests. Instead of having a state government to protect them, the large land holders--especially those of the south--realized that the state government would be indifferent, possibly hostile, to the problems of their class. The southern area of the state was particularly troubled over the tax policies of the state government; they realized that as the mining interests in the North were migratory and seldom settled for a period long enough to be taxed, a great portion of the revenue from a property tax could only come from the taxes on their holdings. Even before California was admitted to the Union, many of the southern rancheros felt that their best interests were separate from those of the northern area. In a petition to Congress signed March 3, 1850, several southern rancheros asked that statehood not be forced upon them, preferring to remain in a territorial status. They claimed that the southern population, being ex-Mexican to more of an extent, was not ready for American institutions and that the proposed area of the state was too large to be governed from a single location. They claimed that statehood would be a cause of financial ruin to them.

> The expenses of the state are, of course, very considerable. . .
> we have been assured that this amount will be enormous. . . .
>
> If any tax be laid on lands, as is customary in other countries,
> it would be the utter ruin of all the properties of the south.[41]

The worst fears of the land holders came true when California was accepted as a state. Not only did the state government resort to a tax on lands for revenue, but it spent money faster than it was able to procure by taxation. The land holders were faced with the prospect of paying for state bonds drawing three per cent per month interest.[42]

One of the troubles that the land holder had to contend with was that of the squatters that swarmed over his land. Instead of finding recourse in the state government, he found that it supported his opponents. The taxes were, to all practical purposes, a weapon to make him settle with the squatter on the terms favorable to the latter; and the large land holder found that the Governor of the state approved of this trend.

> The beneficial effects of a system of direct taxation have already been seen in the increased impulse given to our agriculture during the past year. The large tracts of land have, in many cases, been subdivided and small portions sold to agriculturalists, who have thus become permanent and prosperous residents. [43]

Another ground for dissatisfaction came in 1856 when the state passed legislation which sided with the squatter in his fight with the large land owner. In proposing the law requiring the grant holders to pay for the improvements of the squatters or to sell the land for its appraised value, Governor Bigler made it clear where his interests and sympathies were.

> Of what avail is it that our soil is the most productive, and our climate admirably adapted to the cultivation of all the necessities and luxuries of life, if the flowing vales sleep in native beauty and silence, and expansive plains are but the roaming grounds and rich pasture fields for the unchecked herd? The true wealth of a prolific soil is the hardy and industrious hand which brings it into subjection--which turns the rich sod with the ploughshare, prepares it for the rains of winter and dews at night fall, and which at harvest season, reaps from fields of bending grain the rich recompense of toil. [44]

Although the law was declared unconstitutional in 1857, its passage in the previous year made it clear to the grant holders that they were not going to be protected by a legislative policy. [45]

The large disparity in the taxation and the political control of the northern and southern sections brought more and more of the southern rancheros to hope for separation from the state. In the fiscal year ending June, 1851, the six southern counties with a population of 6,367 had twelve representatives in the state legislature; the twelve northern counties with a population of 119,917 had forty four representatives. The southern counties, however, paid $41,705.26 in taxes, while the northern counties in the same period paid $21,253.66. [46] With a fourth of the political power, the six southern counties were paying in taxes thirty-five times more per citizen than the northern counties.

The movement to divide the state along geographical and economic lines began soon after the admission of California as a state. In Los Angeles a call was made for a convention to divide the state in September, 1851--less than one year after the admission of California. A group of prominent citizens called for the convention on the grounds that legislation was "tending to fasten upon(Southern California) . . . a state of actual oppression which will soon exhaust the energies of a population that deserves a better fate."[47] A bill to separate the six southern counties of the state and form a new territory was passed by the state legislature. The bill was signed by the governor on April 19, 1859 and well over two-thirds of the population of the southern counties approved the measure in an election. A copy of the bill, along with the results of the election, were sent to the President by Senator Broderick. The measure was pigeonholed in Washington and nothing came of it, mainly due to the contorversy over slavery in Congress and the threatening cloud of Civil War.[48]

Certain social customs of the Mexican Californians made the holding of the vast land grants more difficult. No system of land entail was worked out in California. All children, the girls included, could and did inherit in California; and the large families of the Mexican Californians made it difficult to keep the lands intact. Rancho Arroyo de los Pilarcitos was confirmed to Candelario Miramontes for 4,424.12 acres. As the rest of his family soon settled on it, it was soon divided into many pieces. Yet in 1883 Rudolpho Miramontes, one of his sons, still had two hundred and seventy seven acres in San Mateo county and another son, Antonio Miramontes, owned "a beautiful home in Woodside".[49]

With the coming of the Americans, the daughters of the Mexican Californians found a new freedom and many of them insisted upon exercising their new rights. Maria Merced, for example, insisted on managing her own business affairs, even after her marriage to John Rains. Unlike some of her sister Californians who had a good business sense, Maria soon showed that she was completely lost in the business world. Despite the pleas of friends and relatives, she insisted on continuing in her own manner, and by 1867 she had squandered all her lands.[50] The daughters of Francisco Castro were not satisfied with the division of the Rancho San Pablo in Contra Costa county and appealed to the courts--the first of many long expensive litigations that were to eat up most of the estate.[51]

Land changed hands through the women. Sometimes the land stayed in the hands of the Mexican Californians, but merely changed families. Such was the case when the Alvarado family gained control of most of Rancho San Pablo when Juan

Bautista Alvarado married a daughter of Francisco Castro.[52] The Rancho Ballones in Los Angeles county passed from the Machado family to the Lugo family in a similar manner.[53] It was more often, however, that the lands passed by the women into the hands of Americans. The preference of the women for the Anglo-Saxon men of California was so definite that many observers commented on it and tried to explain it.

> There were several reasons why the Spanish California girls were inclined to marry outside their own race. The more sensible and far-seeing of the heads of the old families felt that the future was in the hands of the invading race, that the old easy methods of business and life were no longer of avail and that it was a protection to family interests to have an American son-in-law, one who could give advise in the new business methods, and would have an authentic voice in legal and political affairs. And the girls felt that they acquired prestige by marrying into the dominant race. They were sensible to strange charms . . . and found the foreigners better educated, more worldly wise, than their own countrymen.[54]

This preference developed to such an extent that it overrode the previous sentiments of bitterness developed during the Mexican War and Bear Flag revolt. Dona Augustias de la Guerra was so bitter against the Americans at that time that she hid a fugitive from the Americans in her bed a few days after she had given birth to a child. Yet in later years she followed the example of many of her relatives and friends and married an American, becoming Mrs. William Ord.[55]

The preference of the girls for American men could only lead to one of two results, depending on the characteristics or abilities of the man she married. If the American was able and energetic, the control of the family lands in all probability passed to him. George A. Johnson married a daughter of Francisco Maria Alvarado of San Diego county and by the time the patent was granted for the land in 1873 he had gained control of Rancho Los Penasquitos.[56] Juan Bandini deeded Rancho La Jurupa to his son-in-law Abel Sterns in partial satisfaction for loans of over $24,000 the latter made to him to ease Bandini's financial difficulties.[57] If the husband was not able and energetic, he could be a liability to the Mexican California families. It was to their disadvantage that

> Mostly the native daughters married good looking and outwardly viril but really lazy, worthless, dissolute vagabond Americans whose object of marriage was to get rich without work. . . . Those men squandered their wives' fortunes in all manner of gambling and

dissolute living. . . .[58]

One social condition that weakened the position of the Mexican Californian was the outbreak of insanity in the new state. Antonio Berreyesa in his memoirs says that one of the reasons for the loss of his lands and rancho was the madness brought on by his troubles. He says that the lack of business accumen during this period and his burning of all his documents and records, both induced by his madness, brought about his ruin.[59] Jose Domingo Peralta who, as already has been mentioned, signed a mortgage on Rancho San Ramon thinking it was a lease, died insane in Alameda county in 1876[60] The incidence of insanity was so great that a state institution soon had to be established; yet Vallejo relates that prior to the coming of the Americans, there had only been two cases of insanity in California. He places the cause for the outbreak on the consumption of hard liquor, saying that the native Californians, experienced only to plain "pure" liquors, were not used to the hard liquors introduced by the Germans and the French.[61]

The rancho lands were sold by their owners to an extent that has perhaps been underestimated. Some, it is true, failed to receive but a token payment for the lands, either because they did not understand the value of the land, or else they were in a position where they had to take any offer made. Edward Fitzgerald Beale was able to buy land in Los Angeles county in 1851 for as little as five cents an acre. The land owners seemed to have little idea of the value of the lands that they had received for so little effort and no financial outlay.[62] Manuel Dominguez sold four thousand acres of the San Pedro Rancho for thirty-five cents an acre.[63] Magdalena Estudillo, who was the claimant for Rancho Otay, over sixty-five hundred acres in San Diego county,[64] sold one sixth of her land. Sold at public auction less than five months after she received her patent for the land, it brought thirty-five cents an acre.[65]

Many of the land holders received a good price for their land. The Pacheco family in Contra Costa county had sold parts of the rancho prior to receiving the patent in 1866. Five hundred acres had been sold in 1853 for $3000; six hundred and forty acres were sold for $5000; and another section of the rancho sold for $2,000.[66] When the rancho was finally sold to settle the estate interest of a minor child, it brought $30,000.[67] In northern California the land holders were able to sell much of their lands at a good price. Berreyesa Valley was sold in 1866 for $10,000;[68]

34

in 1854 five thousand acres of the Rancho Santa Rita were sold for $10,000.[69] The Peralta family sold much of their land in Alameda county for good prices. In 1851 W. W. Chipman and Gideon Aughenbaugh bought 2,300 acres of Alameda for $14,000.[70] Vicente Peralta sold the land that the city of Oakland was organized upon for $10,000 in March of 1852.[71] In August of the next year he sold all of Rancho Temescal, except for seven hundred acres, for $100,000.[72] Jose Domingo Peralta sold his ranch, keeping three hundred acres for himself, for a price of $82,000.[73] In southern California the prices were not as high, although some were good. In San Diego county the San Bernardo rancho was sold in 1869 for $36,000, a price of about two dollars an acre.[74] In 1884, the son-in-law of Francisco Maria Alvarado sold Rancho Los Penasquitos for $35,000.[75] In 1874 Ricardo Vejar sold his interest in Rancho San Jose in Los Angeles county for $29,000.[76]

The unsettled business conditions of the new state perilled the enjoyment of the fruits of selling a rancho. The ups and downs of California economics made it difficult to keep a stable fortune intact. Although Clemente Colombet was estimated in 1876 to be worth approximately $300,000 in San Jose, he had lost his rancho lands and a previous fortune in business ventures and then made a second fortune.[77] Jose Maria Amador, one of the first manufacturers and businessmen in California, became embarrassed in his financial affairs in 1852, and had to sell his estates for $22,000.[78] In 1851 Jose del Carmen Lugo had sold his ranch to the Mormons and retired to Los Angeles.[79] He felt that the $77,500 price for the rancho, less its livestock, was sufficient to live comfortably.[80] As Lugo relates in his memoirs, however

> . . . unfortunately I gave my name as security to some persons in whom I had had confidence, and who, for one reason or another left me as they might say vulgarly "on the horns of the bull". I had to sacrifice my property, even the house in which I was living, to meet my obligations.[81]

Salvador Vallejo had lost twelve leagues of his grant to squatters, but was able to sell the remaining four leagues for $160,000. He lost it all, however, in the fall of a banking house in San Francisco and was living in 1874 on the estate of his brother.[82]

Despite the difficulty in obtaining capital, a few of the land holders were able to start subdivisions of their lands. Miguel de Pedrorena was one of the group that tried the unsuccessful move to New San Diego in 1850.[83] The Estudillo family laid out and sold lots in San Lorenzo in 1858 in Alameda county.[84] Mariano Gonzales laid out the town of Gonzales in Monterey county and made enough to be one of the leaders of a narrow gauge railroad from Monterey to Salinas.[85] Juan Bautista Castro laid out Castroville in the Salinas valley. Castro was so concerned with the success of the town that he gave lots to those who could not pay for them in order to insure that his town would have a large population. He failed to realize the importance of the railraod, however, which made Salinas its terminal in the valley, when he haggled over the price of lands for a roundhouse and railroad yard. Instead of Castroville being the center of activity in the valley, Salinas gained that honor through the added impetus of the railroad.[86]

It is true that most of the land soon passed from the hands of the Mexican Californians for one reason or another, but many of the families retained at least a portion of their original estates. While the amount kept under control may not have been even a large percentage of the original holdings, it was often enough to make the owners substantial men in their communities. Fernando Pacheco still owned 1500 acres of the Rancho Monte del Diablo in Contra Costa county in 1882.[87] Francisco Galindo owned 9000 acres of the same grant and was a rancher until 1878 when he built a 250 room hotel in Oakland.[88] Despite the loss of the greater part of their lands in Alameda county, in 1876 "the Estudillo family retained a considerable portion of their original patrimony."[89] Rafael Castro kept control of Rancho Aptos in Santa Cruz county and at his death his estate was described as consisting of the rancho and about $50,000 in bank deposits.[90] The sons of Ignacio Pacheco did well in Marin county. Salvador Pacheco inherited five hundred acres from his father in 1864 and still owned them in 1904.[91] Another son, Gumescindo Pacheco, had his 1006 acres in 1880 in the farming and dairy business.[92] Maria Antonia de la Guerra had married Gaspar Orena and at the death of her father the control of Rancho San Julian in Santa Barbara passed into his capable hands. In 1900 Orena had twenty five homes in Los Angeles, a block of business houses in Santa Barbara, the twenty two thousand acre Rancho Cuyama #1 in San Luis Obispo and Santa Barbara counties, ranchos in San Luis Obispo and Ventura Counties, as well as other property.[93] Despite troubles over loans, Ignacio Machado was able to leave his son nine hundred acres of land, plus 7000 sheep, 50 horses and 100 cattle. In 1907 his son still owned six hundred acres near Benice and Santa Monica.[94]

In those many cases where a descendant of a land grant holder is described in later years as "one of the substantial men of the community. . ."[95] or "one of the most honorable and respected Spanish-American men of the county", [96] it can be assumed that they were able to keep enough of the family lands to insure their influence on the economic and social life of their communities.

In general, if the Mexican Californian did not sell or dispose of his lands during the height of the gold rush, he had a better chance of profiting from his lands if he could keep at least part of them until the 1880's. One reason for this is that the land itself had little value until that time. Grazing land in Los Angeles county was assessed at fifty cents an acre in 1850, but was soon reduced to half that figure. During the drought of 1863 and 1864 the rate was reduced to twelve and one half cents and later to ten cents an acre. [97] Juan Bautista Castro couldn't sell Rancho Bolsa Nueva y Moro Cojo for fifty cents an acre, [98] and land worth from $500 to $2000 dollars an acre in 1885 near San Pedro could not be sold for twenty-five cents an acre in the 1870's. Its owner Ramon D. Sepulveda had to work as a teamster and at other odd jobs to support himself. [99] In some cases a small bit of land that had been kept rose quickly in value due to development of a new area. The laying out of the coast city of Venice caused property values nearby to rise. Vicente Lugo and his sister owned thirteen acres of the land that was once part of the Ballones rancho and they were glad to sell twelve acres of it at $1000 an acre and live on the remainder. [100]

The story of the breakup of the land grants in California is one which has evoked a wide range of feelings and emotions. The lawyer and the jurist feel that the difficulties arose because of a disparity between the Mexican and American methods of legal practice and that the troubles of the Mexican land holders in California were necessary in the establishment of the American juridical system. The economic historian and the sociologist look at this period in another manner.

> If the history of the Mexican grants of California is ever written,
> it will be a history of greed, of perjury, or corruption, of spoilation
> and high handed robbery, for which it will be difficult to find a
> parallel. . . [101]

The citizens of the expanding United States were conscious of the divine mandate to spread the boundaries of the Republic. If they thought at all of the upheaval in the golden promise land of the Pacific Coast, they perhaps explained it in terms of a previous mandate to another chosen people.

I gave you a land on which you had not labored, and cities which you had not built, and you dwell therein; you eat the fruit of vineyards and oliveyards which you did not plant. [102]

In the final analysis, perhaps theirs was the best explanation; for as a group the Mexican land holders in California were unable to make the social and economic changes that the new Promise Land demanded.   The fruits of the land were gathered by a new race.

Footnotes--Chapter II

[1]Proclamation to the People of California on the Third Day of June, 1849, by Governor Bennet Riley (San Francisco, 1942).

[2]John Walton Caughey, California (2nd ed. ; New York, 1953), p. 308.

[3]W. W. Robinson, Land in California (Berkeley, California, 1948), pp. 166-8.

[4]Ibid. , pp. 61 and 112.

[5]Ibid. , p. 112.

[6]Paraphrased from Vicente Perez Rosales, California Adventure (San Francisco, 1943), p. 68.

[7]Caughey, op. cit. , p. 308.

[8]Walter Colton, Three Years in California (New York, 1850), pp. 359-60.

[9]Speeches of Mr. Gwin in the Senate of the United States on Private Land Titles in the State of California (Washington, 1851), p. 35.

[10]Caughey, op. cit. , pp. 314-5; Robinson, op. cit. , p. 146.

[11]William W. Morrow, Spanish and Mexican Private Land Grant Cases (San Francisco, 1923), p. 27.

[12]Robinson, op. cit. , p. 5.

[13]Horace Bell, On The Old West Coast (New York, 1930), p. 5.

[14]John S. Hottell, "Mexican Land Grants in California," Hutchings' Illustrated Californian Magazine (1857-58), II, p. 442.

[15]Caughey, op. cit. , p. 309.

[16]Morrow, op. cit. , p. 14.

[17]Ogden Hoffman, Report of Land Cases Determined in the United States District Court for the Northern District of California (San Francisco, 1862), Appendix.

[18]Ibid.

[19]Carey McWilliams, North From Mexico (New York, 1949), pp. 91-2.

[20]Robert Glass Cleland, The Cattle on a Thousand Hills (2nd. ed. ; San Marino, California, 1951), p. 102.

[21] Fred W. Atkinson, One Hundred Years in Pajaro Valley, From 1769 to 1869 (Watsonville, California, 1935), p. 14.

[22] Anne B. Fisher, The Salinas; Upside-down River (New York, 1945), pp. 174-5.

[23] San Francisco Bulletin, July 1, 1876; San Francisco Chronicle, March 26, 1879.

[24] William Halley, The Centenial Year Book of Alameda County, California (Oakland, California, 1876), p. 552.

[25] Frank Clinton Merritt, History of Alameda County, (Chicago, 1928), I, p. 79.

[26] John Francis Sheenan Jr., "The Story of the San Pablo Rancho", Overland Monthly, XXIV (July-December, 1894), pp. 517-23.

[27] Mae Fisher Purcel, History of Contra Costa County (Berkeley, California, 1940), p. 138.

[28] Ibid., p. 192.

[29] Fisher, op. cit., pp. 159-60.

[30] Robinson, op. cit., pp. 85-7; Hoffman, op. cit., Appendix, p. 48.

[31] Robinson, op. cit., pp. 41-2.

[32] Bell, op. cit., p. 9.

[33] Ibid., pp. 8-10.

[34] Fisher, op. cit., p. 132.

[35] Cleland, op. cit., p. 132.

[36] Ibid., p. 136.

[37] Mariano E. Gonzales, "Statement", Manuscript in Bancroft Library, Berkeley, California.

[38] Fisher, op. cit., p. 171-5.

[39] James Miller Guinn, A History of California; and an Extended History of its Southern Coast Counties (Los Angeles, 1907), pp. 457-8.

[40] Ibid., p. 268.

[41] Mary M. Bowman, "California State Division Controversy", Historical Society of Southern California Annual Publication, X, Part III (1919), p. 76.

[42] John Bigler, _Annual Message of the Governor, 1856_ (n. p., 1856), p. 9.

[43] Peter H. Burnett, _Annual Message of the Governor, 1851_ (San Jose, 1851), p. 19.

[44] Bigler, op. cit., p. 24.

[45] Billings vs. Hall (1857), 7 Cal 1.

[46] John McDougal, "Annual Message of the Governor, 1852", in _Journal of the Third Session of the Senate of the State of California_ (San Francisco, 1852), p. 12.

[47] Bowman, op. cit., p. 78.

[48] William Henry Ellison, "The Movement for State Division in California, 1849-1860", _Texas State Historical Association Quarterly,_ XVII (October, 1913), pp. 133-5.

[49] _History of San Mateo, California; Including its Geography, Topography, Geology, Climatology and Description_ (San Francisco, 1883), pp. 299-301; Hoffman, op. cit., Appendix, p. 49.

[50] George William Beattie and Helen Hunt Beattie, _Heritage of the Valley_ (Oakland, California, 1951), pp. 148, 169.

[51] Sheenan, op. cit., pp. 513--23.

[52] Purcel, op. cit., pp. 137-8.

[53] Guinn, _Southern Coast Counties_, p. 1132.

[54] Bell, op. cit., p. 257.

[55] Augustias de la Guerra Ord, "Occurencias en California", Manuscript in Bancroft Library, Berkeley, California.

[56] Robert W. Brackett, _A History of the Ranchos_ (San Diego, California, 1939), p. 22.

[57] Cleland, op. cit., p. 197.

[58] Bell, op. cit., p. 256.

[59] Antonio Berreyesa, "Memorias". Manuscript in Bancroft Library, Berkeley, California, pp. 8-18.

[60] _San Francisco Bulletin,_ July 1, 1876; _San Francisco Chronicle,_ March 26, 1879.

[61] Mariano G. Vallejo, "Historia de California". Manuscript in Bancroft Library, Berkeley, California, vol. 5, pp. 238-9.

[62] Helen S. Giffen and Arthur Woodward, The Story of El Tejon (Los Angeles, 1942), p. 45.

[63] Guinn, Southern Coast Counties, p. 397.

[64] Hoffman, op. cit., appendix, p. 60.

[65] San Diego Union, June 7, 1872.

[66] L. C. Wittenmeyer, Abstract of Title to the Lands in Rancho San Ramon, Contra Costa County, California (San Francisco, 1874), pp. 1-10.

[67] Ibid., p. 13-5.

[68] C. A. Menefee, Historical and Descriptive Sketch Book of Napa, Sonoma, Lake and Mendocino (Napa City, California, 1873), p. 146.

[69] Halley, op. cit., p. 501.

[70] Roy C. Beckman, The Romance of Oakland (Oakland, California, 1932), p. 11.

[71] Halley, op. cit., p. 450.

[72] Merritt, op. cit., I, pp. 109-10.

[73] Ibid.

[74] Brackett, op. cit., pp. 51-2.

[75] Ibid., p. 22.

[76] Guinn, Southern Coast Counties, p. 391.

[77] Manuel Torres, "Peripecias de la Vida Californiana". Manuscript in Bancroft Library, Berkeley, California, p. 82.

[78] Merritt, op. cit., I, p. 67.

[79] Jose de Carmen Lugo, "Vida de un Ranchero". Manuscript in Bancroft Library, Berkeley, California.

[80] Beattie, op. cit., p. 88.

[81] Lugo, op. cit.

[82] Jose Maria Salvador Vallejo, "Notas Historicas Sobre California". Manuscript in Bancroft Library, Berkeley, California, p. 152-5.

[83] Brackett, op. cit., pp. 64-6.

[84] Alameda Tax Book (Eden Township), 1858, pp. 58-9.

[85] Gonzales, op. cit.

[86] Fisher, op. cit., pp. 194-220.

[87] F. P. Munro-Frazer, History of Contra Costa County, California (San Francisco, 1882), pp. 629-30.

[88] James Miller Guinn, History of the State of California and Biographical Record of Oakland and Environs (Los Angeles, 1907), p. 855.

[89] Halley, op. cit., p. 477.

[90] Sacramento Record Union, May 18, 1878; San Jose Pioneer, June 1, 1878.

[91] James Miller Guinn, A History of the State of California and Biographical Record of the Coast Counties (Chicago, 1904), p. 765.

[92] F. P. Munro-Frazer, History of Marin County, California (San Francisco, 1880), p. 443.

[93] James Miller Guinn, Historical and Biographical Record of Southern California (Chicago, 1902), p. 988.

[94] Guinn, Southern Coast Counties, pp. 925-6.

[95] James Miller Guinn, History of the State of California and Biographical Record of Santa Cruz, San Benito, Monterey, and San Louis Obispo Counties (Chicago, 1903), p. 466.

[96] Munro-Frazer, Marin County, p. 418; Guinn, Coast Counties, p. 929; Los Angeles Herald, April 4, 1880; Menefee, op. cit., pp. 182-3.

[97] Cleland, op. cit., pp. 135-6, 119.

[98] Fisher, op. cit., p. 164.

[99] Roman D. Sepulveda, "Dictation". Manuscript in Bancroft Library, Berkeley, California.

[100] Guinn, Southern Coast Counties, p. 1132.

[101] Henry George, Our Land and Land Policy, National and State (New York, 1911), p. 39.

[102] Joshua 24: 13.

CHAPTER III

THE BATTLE OF THE BALLOTS:

THE MEXICAN-AMERICAN IN CALIFORNIA POLITICS,

1850-1875

One of the main problems facing the new American citizens of Mexican background in California in the period of 1849 to 1875 was their adaptation to the new
political system. Although their period as a Mexican territory should have given
them some experience in self-government, the distance from the center of government, the apathy or inability of that government to give attention to their problems,
and a distinct regional consciousness, all helped to bring about some attempts at
self-government during that period. Whatever the reasons, the Mexican-Americans
seemingly were able to adapt quickly to the new political ways and to use them to
protect their special interests. The north-south split in California politics began
early; and as the main stronghold of the Mexican-Americans was in Southern California, this conclusion seemingly is valid. Carey McWilliams has been content with
this conclusion, and feels that politics in California in the period 1849 to 1870 was
based on this racial division. [1]

If the north-south split in California politics was racial in its origin, then the
best place that the Mexican- Americans would have to insure their position would be
at the State Constitutional Convention in 1849. There the Americans would be willing
to bargain in order to fulfill their intense desire to become a state. The Mexican-
Americans from Southern California were doubtful of the wisdom of joining the northern
section in statehood, and would be in a good bargaining position. When the vote was
taken on whether or not the convention was to ask for territorial or statehood status,
all of the Mexican-American delegates voted for territorial status, with the excep-
tion of Mariano G. Vallejo--who was the only Mexican American delegate from
Northern California. [2] The Convention itself gave the Mexican-Americans an advantage; as most of the committees had members from each district, the Mexican-
Americans often were given a representation not in proportion to their numbers in
California. For example, on the Standing Committee on the Constitution there were
two members from each of the ten districts, with six of the twenty members--or
thirty percent--being Mexican Americans. [3] The Seventh Census in 1850 gave the

44

total Spanish speaking population of California as approximately fifteen percent.[4] The Mexican-Americans, therefore, were in a better position numerically to obtain those concessions they wanted.

By looking at the record of the Convention proceedings, it is possible to see just what the Mexican-American delegates wanted. One of the few definite stands that were made by these delegates was for the right of the Indians to vote. Under the leadership of Pablo de la Guerra, they claimed that many of the Indians were capable of voting and being intelligent citizens; that many of them had been taxpayers under the Mexican government, and that they had been pushed to a low level by their later virtual enslavement. The Mexican-American delegates wanted those Indians who were able to vote to be given the right, and not be disfranchised by the constitution. Finally the state legislature was given the power to grant the franchise to those Indians they considered capable of using it; this compromise was proposed by Pablo de la Guerra.[5] The proposal to require that all laws be published in Spanish and English was held to be unnecessary by many of the American delegates, but was passed as a measure to still the fears of the Spanish speaking citizens.[6] In proposing that the appellate jurisdiction be restricted to matters of $200 or more, de la Guerra faced considerable opposition from many of the northern California delegates who held that constitutional problems were often settled by cases of small financial importance. A native California characteristic was described when de la Guerra explained the reasons for his proposal.

> Among many of the reasons which I have for proposing the amendment, the principal one is that very often there are rich persons who do not care so much about the decision of the case on account of the amount involved in it, but who make use of their wealth to carry out their caprices. . . I have known persons to appeal merely on the subject of a calf, and send it up to the Supreme Court of Mexico. . . to gratify a malicious feeling towards the opposite party.[7]

This too was finally written into the Constitution, and concludes the proposals of the Mexican-American delegates.

The stand of the delegates on proposals made by the other delegates which affected them gives also an insight into what the Mexican-Americans did and did not want. J. F. Lippitt, representing San Francisco, proposed that entailed estates be made impossible.

I have a very short section to offer here: <u>No perpetulties shall</u>

> be allowed. It is to prevent perpetuity of lands from families to
> families. It is upon perpetuities that aristocracies are built
> upon. [8]

As entailed estates were not common in California--the women being heirs even made passing of an estate for a few generations difficult--the section was passed without debate.

Some of the brightest verbal fireworks of the Convention occurred over the question of whether or not to continue the community property system which enabled the wife to keep separate the property she had when she entered marriage. The question was drawn on the position of women's rights and that of common law. Some attacked the community property clause on the grounds that it subverted the common law, the basis of all American legal institutions. For this stand, J. M. Jones of San Joaquin has a fervent rebuttal.

> Sir, I want no such system; the inhabitants of this country want no
> such thing; the Americans of this country want no such thing. They
> want a code of simple laws which they can understand; no common
> law, full of exploded principles, with nothing to recommend it but
> some dog latin, or the opinions of some lawyer who lived a hundred
> years ago; they want something the people can comprehend. . .
> Where is this common law which we must revert to? Has the gentle-
> man from Monterey got it? Can he produce it? Did he ever see
> it?. . . I am an advocate of all such law as the people can under-
> stand. Whether I find it in that book or this, I say let us give to
> the people, who have been chained down for hundreds of years,
> the right and privilege of understanding their own laws. I would
> make the laws. . . so plain, simple, and comprehensible, that
> every man. . . could go into a court of law and defend himself
> . . . [9]

It was in the matter of the rights of women that the oratorial phrases become the heaviest; and the community property clause was viewed as attacking the very relationship of the sexes.

> Sir, the god of nature made women frail, lovely, and dependent;
> and such the common law pronounces her. Nature did what the
> common law has done--put her under the protection of man. . .
> He who would not let the winds of heaven too rudely touch her, is
> her best protection. When she trusts him with her happiness, she
> may as well trust him with her gold. . . This doctrine of women's
> rights, is the doctrine of those mental hermaphrodites, Abbey Folsom,
> Fanney Wright, and the rest of that tribe. [10]

Those who defended the clause on the grounds of women's rights attacked the position of the woman under the common law as a relic of the dark ages and that modern society gave her certain rights and privileges.

The most telling argument for the community property clause, and the one which probably brought its final acceptance, was a practical one. In the words of H. A. Teft of San Luis Obispo:

> The industrious businessman, with his frugal wife, is not in any way affected by it; but if an idle, dissipated, visionary, or impractical man brings his family to penury or want, than I say it is our duty to put this provision in the Constitution for the protection of that family who are helpless, and who have no other means of subsistence. [11]

> I claim that it is due to every wife, and to the children of every family, that the wife's property shall be protected; and I am not willing to trust the Legislature in this matter. [12]

The leaders in the convention for the Community property were not the Mexican-Americans, but Americans representing areas where there were large numbers of Mexican-Americans; H. A. Teft of San Luis Obispo, K. H. Dimmick of San Jose, and J. M. Jones of San Joaquin. [13] A conclusion that might be drawn is that the Mexican-American interests were capably represented by the delegates from their district not of their race. This in turn brings doubt upon the thesis that the north-south split in California politics was primarily racial in origin. Might not the southern Californians have more common economic ties among themselves than racial differences?

The land owner vs. merchant split in California politics came into the open when the Convention came to the problem of taxation. When the proposition was made that the job of assessor be made an elective one in each county. F. T. Lippit of San Francisco expressed the fear that such a practice in counties with large land owners would only encourage fraud and deception. It was on this subject that Pablo de la Guerra made one of his few speeches of the convention.

> I desire to make a few observations in regard to what the gentleman has said. He appeared to be afraid that in some districts one or two large land owners may have the power of naming as assessor whatever person they like; and that those being nominated by their influence would value the property as the owners would direct. . . I am not acquainted with this means of appraising property for the purpose of taxation, for it has never been customary in California;

but I understand that when a merchant is called upon, his oath
is taken as to the value of his property. If a merchant's oath
is to be taken, why cannot a land owner's be taken? I do not
see why bad faith should be expected from one class of persons
more than another?[14]

The north-south economic split continued, reaching its climax in the attempts to divide the state. Even before California was admitted as a state, a group of southern Californians asked that the southern portion of California be separated from the rest and be made a separate political division. Within a year of California's admission as a state, a convention was called at Los Angeles to begin proceedings to divide the state. The main grievance of the southern Californians was that their larger taxable wealth and smaller population made them an easy prey for the northern Californians with whom they were coupled. They claimed that their economic interests were best served by severence from northern California. To underline that the grievances were economic rather than racial, among the leaders of the movement were such southern California ranchers as Benjamin Hayes, J. Lancaster Brent, Lewis Granger, and John O. Wheeler.[15]

If the north-south split in California politics was not primarily racial in its origin, perhaps the Mexican-Americans were able to use this split to maintain their social and economic position in southern California. If they tried to do so, a glance at the list of state offices filled by Mexican-Americans shows that they were not strikingly successful.[16] It is true, however, that California politics in the period 1850 to 1875 gave them ample opportunity to try. During that period, only twice was a political party able to win two successive elections for the governorship; the Democrats in the period 1858 to 1862 and the Republicans in the period 1862 to 1867.[17] It is significant to note that most of the campaign literature in Spanish falls into two categories. If the election was to be close, the issues pertained especially to the Mexican-Americans; otherwise, the campaign literature was just a translation of the literature in English.

In 1856 the Republicans made a shrewd bid for support of the Mexican-Americans in California for their presidential candidate, John C. Fremont. In an appeal in Spanish the Republicans called upon both the pride of race and the economic interests of the Mexican-Americans in California.

. . . he is the person who in Cahuenga, alone on horseback, rode
through our camp to confer with Don Andres Pico. . . (saying to

48

his friends) "I know well the character of the Californians better than you gentlemen. They are brave and trustworthy, they are not so treasonable. . ."

Also, he is the man who has always been our friend. He wants you to have a railroad from this state to those of the Atlantic; to improve the value of your lands, and facilitate your business and pleasure. [18]

The effect of the appeal was mirrored in the comments of the press of the day.

. . . (Los Angeles) county is divided between Buchanan and Fremont; the Monte Americans, chiefly from Texas and Arkansas, the Germans, and about half of the Americans of the place favoring Buchanan; while the Native Californians, the French and the other half of the Americans of the place uphold Fremont. The vote of the county will be nearly equally divided.

Last year the Monte Americans were all for the American ticket; this year they are for Buchanan. Last year the Californians voted the Democratic ticket but this year they are against it. [19]

In the election of 1860, the Lecompton Democrats won by a two to one majority, electing the governor, twenty-eight of the thirty state senators and seventy of the eighty members of the lower house. [20] In such a landslide the minority had no room to bargain. In the election of 1864 the Republican or Union party was able to use a three fold appeal to the Mexican-Americans. First, it was able to blame the Mexican War on the Democratic party as a plot to gain more slave territory for the South. Secondly, it could blame the Land Act of 1851 upon Democratic Senator William Gwin; and third, it could claim that any help for Mexico against the French intervention of the time, could only come from themselves. [21] But because of the strength of the party in California (they won the gubernatorial election of 1862 by over half again as many votes as the next party[22]) they did not have to make special concessions or promises.

In the election for governor in 1867, the Republicans again played the Union party label for its vote catching appeal; the Mexican counsul in San Francisco took part in a reception for the Union party candidate. The party press hoped that ". . . (his example) will not be without. . . influence in rallying the Mexican population to the support of the union ticket in California."[23] The Democratic party made a concerted effort for the Mexican-American vote. Henry H. Haight, as candidate for governor, promised to do all he could to quickly end the litigation over land titles

49

so that the Mexican-Americans "as legitimate owners" could have peaceful possession of clear title. He further proposed to back the southern route railroad as the "only practical route."[24] The southern railroad was one of the main Democratic promises to the voters of Southern California. It was "to open a new horizon in the future of Southern California."[25] In Los Angeles the Weekly Republican had to console its readers that at least the election showed that the traditional Democratic majority in the county had declined.[26]

By election of 1868 there were clear indications that the Mexican-American block of votes had failed to materialize. By far the most important reason was that there were not enough to make a substantial vote. In the census of 1850, the total Spanish speaking population was less than 15%--even including all those born in Mexico, Spain, South and Central American and counting all born in California in this category.[27] It is difficult to estimate the percentage in any later census, because it is impossible to tell what percentage of those born in California were of Mexican-American parentage. But with the assumption that the original Mexican-American families maintained their numbers, the percentage of the population--again including those born in Mexico, Spain and South and Central America--was no more than twelve percent in 1860 and four percent in 1870.[28] Although these figures are only rough approximations, they are enough to show that the Mexican-American population in no way maintained a growth equal to that of the entire state.

The Mexican-Americans failed to become a power as a group in politics. The majority of the Mexican-Americans were Democrats because they were from Southern California, and their regional interests were best represented by that party. Southern California was not Democratic because of the Mexican-Americans; the Mexican-Americans from Southern California were Democrats as were the majority of their neighbors. But even within the Democratic party in Southern California, the Mexican-Americans soon lost importance to other racial groups. By the election of 1868, the appeal of the Democratic press was directed to the interests of the German, Irish, and other foreign born citizens. The Know-Nothing backgrounds of Frank M. Pixley, the Republican candidate for Congress, and of Schulyer Colfax, the candidate for Vice-President, were exploited.[29] Even much of the appeal to the Roman Catholics was slanted toward the Irish and not the Spanish-speaking population.[30]

One of the first signs that the Mexican-Americans were not going to be a major factor in California politics was the rapid growth of the Know-Nothing party in California, culminating with its control of the state in the election of the governor from 1856 to 1858.[31]

> . . . the anti-foreign agitation was not directed against the Spaniards and Orientals, although these constituted an alarming number of the population of California. The Know-Nothings were opposed to undue political <u>influence</u> on the part of foreign-born citizens. . . whereas the Spaniards and Orientals were of little political influence.[32]

A comment by Mariano G. Vallejo discloses the relative political importance of racial groups in northern California. Vallejo pointed out that French and German were taught in the San Francisco schools because these two groups could produce 30,000 votes; as the Hispanic-Americans could only muster 4,000 votes, Spanish was not part of the curriculum.[33]

The political career of Romualdo Pacheco culminated in his serving as Governor of the state for almost a year; and as a member of a Mexican-American family, his life and career merit more than a passing glance. With anything more than that glance, however, his success cannot be attributed to a "typical" Mexican-American. At the age of five, he was sent to the Hawaiian Islands to school; when he returned at the age of twelve, he had forgotten his native Spanish. His mother had remarried and the young boy was apprenticed on board the ship of his step-father John Wilson.[34] In his political life, he soon turned to the Republican party, despite the predominance of the Democratic party in his native in Southern California.

Pacheco served from 1858 to 1859 as State Senator from San Luis Obispo and Santa Barbara in the 9th and 10th Legislatures, having been elected as a Democrat. At the ourbreak of the Civil War, he was again elected and served from 1862 to 1863 as a Union Democrat. With a few strokes of the imagination it is easy to fill in the reasons for the rest of his success. In the election of 1863, the Union party was looking for some means to back its claim of non-partisanship during the war; Pacheco was a logical choice. He had shown his willingness to work for the Union; he was from Southern California; he carried a Spanish name. As the citizens of Southern California had always complained of the tax policies of the state, to nominate Pacheco for the position of State Treasurer increased his political value to the state ticket. The tactics were so successful that Pacheco was nominated for reelection in 1867; the Democrats in in turn nominated Antonio F. Coronel of Los Angeles. Although defeated in 1867, Pacheco showed his vote-getting powers by winning a seat in the 18th Legislature as a Republican State senator from 1869 to 1870. Such campaign appeal in a party member could not pass "unrewarded" and Pacheco was nominated and elected Lt. Governor in 1871. When Governor Newton Booth resigned to take the post of U. S. Senator, Pacheco finished out the term as governor.[35] In his life and career, then, Romualdo Pacheco, although one of the most successful Mexican-Americans, cannot be called representative. His success, in great part, can be attributed to the fact that his political beliefs were different from most Mexican-Americans.

The thesis that the political split between northern and southern California was radial in its origin lacks any substantial proof. Even the assumption that the Mexican-Americans profited politically from that split, to protect their special interests, is doubtful. Their lack of numbers made dominance, even in Southern California, an impossibility in Times, of close elections, special efforst were made to gain the Mexican-Amharic vote. Even then, the appeals were usually regional rather than radial; the campaign promises translated from Spanish to English would often appeal to the neighbor of the Mexican-American. The political importance of the Mexican-Americans, then, depended on how important the small segment of the total vote represented by the Mexican-Americans might be. This conclusions, while perhaps distasteful to the Mexican-American apoligist, is more in conformity with political reality.

52

[1] Carey McWilliams, North From Mexico (New York, 1949), p. 92.

[2] J. Ross Browne, Report on the Debates in the Convention of California on the Formation of the State Constitution in September and October of 1849 (Washington, 1850), pp. 21-23.

[3] Ibid., p. 29.

[4] Born in California, 6602; in Spain, 220; in Mexico, 6454; in Central America, 39; in South America, 877; (total 14,192); Seventh Census, 1850 (Washington, 1854) pp. 116-118. Ibid., p. 972 gives the California population born therein as 7765, which would make the total Spanish speaking population 15,355 in a total population of 92,597. These figures do not include San Francisco, Santa Clara, and Contra Costa counties.

[5] Browne, op. cit., pp. 305-323 and Appendix, p. iv.

[6] Ibid., pp. 273-274.

[7] Ibid., p. 225.

[8] Ibid., p. 272. In its final form as Article XI, section 16, the words "except for elementary purposes" were added. See Ibid., Appendix, p. xi.

[9] Ibid., p. 258.

[10] Ibid., p. 260.

[11] Ibid., p. 259.

[12] Ibid., p. 258.

[13] Ibid., pp. 257-269.

[14] Ibid., p. 365.

[15] Mary M. Bowman, "California State Division Controversy", Historical Society of Southern California Annual Publication, X, part III (1911), pp. 76-78.

[16] See Appendix B.

[17] H. D. Barrows, "Governors of California", Historical Society of Southern California Annual Publication, VI (1906), pp. 32-36.

[18] "A los Nativos Californios", Society of California Pioneers Publication, XXIII (1941), pp. 42-43.

[19] San Francisco Daily Evening Bulletin, October 28, 1856.

[20] California Blue Book, or State Roster, 1911, (Sacramento, 1913). See Appendix B.

[21] "Reflecciones a los Californios e Hispano-Americanos sobre la eleccion presidencial de 1864, por su amigo V. Dartin" (San Francisco, n. d.).

[22] Barrows, op. cit.

[23] Los Angeles Weekly Republican, August 31, 1857.

[24] "Alocucion que dirije a los hijos del Pais H. H. Haight, Nominado por el Partido Democratico para Gobernador de Estado" (n. p. (1867?), pp. 2-3.

[25] "Alocucion de Samuel B. Axtell, Candidato nominado por el Partido Democratico para el Congreso Federal, por el Pr. Distrito de California, que dirije a los nativos Californios y a los Hispano-Americanos" in Haight, "Alocucion . . .", p. 7.

[26] Los Angeles Weekly Republican, September 7, September 14, 1867.

[27] See Footnote No. 3.

[28] In 1860 the free population was 379,994. Of the foreign born in California 100 were from Central America; 2,250 from South America; 470 from Spain; and 9,150 from Mexico. 8th Census, 1860, Statistics. . . in 1860, pp. li, liii, and liv. In 1870 the total population was 560,247, or 582,031 if Indians not taxed are included. Of the foreignborn population 124 were from Central America; 1,956 from South America; 405 from Spain; and 9,339 from Mexico. 9th Census, 1870, Statistics. . . in 1870, pp. xvii, 338, and 341-2.

[29] Los Angeles News, September 22, October 30, 1868.

[30] Ibid. , October 2, 1868.

[31] Barrows, op. cit.

[32] Peyton Hurt, The Rise and Fall of the "Know-Nothings" in California (San Francisco, 1930), pp. 64-5.

[33] Mariano G. Vallejo, "Historia de California" (Unpublished Manuscript in Bancroft Library, Berkeley, California, p. 240.

[34] Hubert Howe Bancroft, History of California (San Francisco, 1884-90), VII, p. 406.

[35] California Blue Book, pp. 222, 314, and 420.

CHAPTER IV

THE COMMON CAUSE OF LIBERALISM:
THE MEXICAN-AMERICAN AND CALIFORNIA OPINION
TOWARD FRENCH INTERVENTION IN MEXICO, 1861-1867

One of the many problems that complicated the early days of the Lincoln administration in 1861 was that of the American foreign policy toward the trouble ridden nation of Mexico. There was little doubt as to the position the United States would have liked to take, but the position of the State Department in Mexican relations was inmeshed with the internal problems of the United States. That Secretary of State William H. Seward was able to influence the withdrawal of French forces from Mexico by negotiation alone is one of this major achievements. His success is all the more noteworthy when it is realized that he not only had to fight against the national pride and interests of France, but also against a growing faction at home that demanded an immediate solution and who were willing to use force if necessary.

It would be natural to assume that among the leaders of this faction would be those citizens in California who had been Mexican citizens before the annexation of that area into the Union. The study of the part California played in the agitation against Seward's Mexican policy gives an insight into the adaptation of the Mexicans into American society in California.

The American policy toward Mexico from 1861 to 1865 was tempered with the knowledge that the United States could not take a decisive stand until her own internal problems were solved. The United States refused to act with England, Spain and France in their intervention to press the claims of their citizens; the administration even seriously considered a loan to Mexico to enable her to make the payments to these foreign powers. When France alone continued the program of intervention, Seward expressed to the American minister to France the only practical stand the United States could make at that time:

> France has a right to make war against Mexico, and to determine for herself the cause. We have a right and interest to insist that France shall not improve the war she makes to raise up in Mexico an anti-republican or anti-American government, or to maintain such a government there. . . .

We do not wish to surpress the fact that our sympathies are with

Mexico, and our wishes are for the restoration of peace within her
borders. . . . We may have our own opinions about the necessity
or the expediency of the movements. . . of France. . . . But we
are not called upon to retain which. . . we have no right and no
present occasion to enforce. [1]

This was the position that the United States maintained until her internal affairs

improved. This policy was motivated by the fear that the Confederacy would other-

wise be recognized by France; it was based on the assumption by 1862 that the French

would never find "real submission" or "practical acquiescence" in Mexico. [2] The

conclusion of the American Civil War made it possible for the Department of State

to take a more determined attitude toward the Mexican policy of Napoleon III, and

by the end of 1865 he found his position there both unprofitable and untenable diplo-

matically. Early in 1866 Napoleon announced the gradual withdrawal of French

forces from Mexico. [3]

In California, the citizens of Mexican descent were able to show their

feelings soon after the intervention by the European powers. A Spanish newspaper,

La Voz de Mejico, was founded early in 1862 and, as its name implied, its claim

was to be the voice of the Mexicans in California. Soon after its inception it called

for the formation of juntas of patriotic citizens throughout California to help Mexi-

co. [4] The arrival of the steamship Oregon on the evening of March 21, 1864, brought

to California a more practical way of aiding Mexico. The next day La Voz de Mejico

announced the arrival of Citizen General Placido Vega, Constitutional Governor of

the State of Sinaloa. [5] Late in 1862 the American Minister in Mexico had observed

that "If the Mexican government had money to maintain and equip troops, it could

easily bring into the field fifty thousand effective men. But they have neither money

nor arms. . ." [6] Money would continue to be a problem, but General Vega had

come to California in an attempt to obtain arms for his government. In his actions

for the Juarez government, he was to provide a catalyst around which public opin-

ion could be formed in California.

General Vega was commissioned to draw $260,000 from the Custom houses

at Mazatlan and Guaymas, to proceed to San Francisco or any other city in the United

States that he might deem advisable, and to purchase arms and munitions for the

Mexican army. He was told to investigate the possibility of sending the arms by

land, as ocean shipments would be more easily traced and, therefore, more easily

a source of embarrassment to the United States Government. The instructions

pointed out, however, that even if it means a loss of time, the primary consideration was "the best, or better yet, complete security."[7] Vega was able to purchase
some arms before he left Mexico: by March of 1864, the Minister of War had
received 8854 rifles from Vega with others being negotiated for.[8] Among the
weapons later purchases were two types of Prussian muskets, some English Enfield
rifles, and the same model Springfield rifle then in use by the United States Army.[9]
Before returning to Mexico, General Vega spent almost $620,000 on his commis-
sion.[10]

There were two main troubles that plagued Vega in his attempts to obtain
arms in California. The first was the lack of funds at his command; the second was
the arms embargo, a result of the neutral policy of the United States government.
In his attempts to solve these problems with aid from California, Vega found that for
various reasons the Mexican people in California were not to be his main supporters.
He soon found that the Mexicans and those of Mexican extraction could or would not
help him. More than once General Vega must have echoed the words of one of the
junta leaders in Mariposa county:

> . . . this place is plagued with an epidemic of men without hearts,
> without honor, without love of country. . . the few Mexicans there
> are, are for the most part conservative--or what is the same thing,
> they do not sympathize with our sacred cause.[11]

There were several reasons why the Mexicans and those of Mexican descent
did not help Vega as much as he expected. The first was that the Mexicans simply
did not have the money he needed; the Mexican-Americans who did, were more
closely identified with the interests of the Americans than with the Mexicans.
Secondly, the group that Vega had relied upon had little means of molding public
opinion. The main reason, however, was that an active role was soon taken over
by a portion of the American population. Rather than looking at the efforts of the
Mexicans and Mexican-Americans, a truer picture is obtained when the efforts of
California are viewed as a whole.

La Voz de Mejico printed lists of contributors who gave for the support of
the liberal cause in Mexico; during 1863 and 1864 the average monthly contribution
from all of California was around $500.[12] Most of the money raised was sent to
Mexico; only once was it turned over to Vega, when he received $1000 in mid-1864.[13]
The usual contribution was one dollar or less, and seldom went up as high as five

dollars. The great majority of contributions came from Mexican citizens; Californians of Mexican descent who gave were listed separately, as were those from South and Central American countries.[14] The poverty of the Mexicans kept them from volunteering to fight in Mexico; many of those who did volunteer lacked the resources to travel to San Francisco.[15] Those Mexican-Californians who had money and prestige had it mainly because as a class they had large land holdings. Unfortunately, because of the drought of 1863-64, these people were in a period of economic transition and unable to meet the appeals by Vega; they were of more value to him for what they could do for him than for what they could give him. Mariano G. Vallejo planned to help Vega obtain a ship in 1865 to transport his arms; as one of Vega's main problems was arranging for transportation without attracting the attention of the French consul and the military authorities, this aid was probably more welcome than any financial help that Vallejo could have made at that time.[16] Romualdo Pacheco placed an ad in the Sacramento Union for fifteen days at the request of General Vega, but his support, within the Republican party as State Treasurer of California was of far greater importance.[17] Salvio Pacheco contributed $200, but along with Augustin Alviso and Victor Castro he was able to collect $24,000 from the businessmen of San Francisco. In his official report Vega lists some $209,000 in contributions, of which $192,000 can be definitely attributed to the business interests of San Francisco and San Diego. W. H. L. Barnes, by contributing professional services valued at almost $4000, made a larger contribution than any Mexican or Mexican-American listed.[18] The money that financed the special commission in California to purchase arms, came not from the Mexicans and Mexican-Americans in California, but from the American businessmen of the state.

In the matter of forming public opinion, the Juarez partisan hopes in California would be severely hampered if they relied primarily on the Spanish speaking element. While Vega was in San Francisco, three newspapers were being published in Spanish: El Nuevo Mundo, El Eco del Pacifico, and La Voz de Mejico. Even these newspapers did not present a solid front for Vega's efforts; he was accused of treason in a letter in El Eco del Pacifico and had to press libel charges to clear his name.[19] More of a disadvantage was the fact that these newspapers did not reach the majority of Californians, who spoke only English. Because of the reactionary position of the Roman Catholic hierarchy in Mexico and their conflict with the liberalism of Juarez, the Catholic press and hierarchy in California, which otherwise might have helped in forming favorable opinion, was lost to the Juarez sympathizers. The effects of an adverse comment on the affairs in Mexico in a pastoral letter on another subject were felt in the editorial columns of La Voz de Mejico.[20] When the same newspaper accused the Mexican clergy of treason and apostacy as well as other crimes "committed in the name of God and for the holy interests of the land and investments of the Church", the result could only be further alienation of a majority of the clergy in California.[21]

Despite these facts, the efforts of Matias Romero, the Mexican Minister to the United States, of Placido Vega, and of the various consuls in the United States were successful in bringing the United States' active aid to their country.

Before his arrival in the United States Vega had expressed the opinion "that despite the military order of the War Department in Washington against exporting them, it will not be difficult for us to obtain some (arms), because of the favor of those in authority with our cause."[22] Vega was mistaken, at least during the Civil War. Romero was to complain that the French were allowed to purchase mules and wagons in the United States for their army in Mexico, while the Mexicans were not allowed to purchase the one thing that would help them--arms and munitions. The position of the United States, entirely unsatisfactory to the Mexican government, was that the mules and wagons were not covered under the rules of contraband, and that unfortunately the internal condition of the United States necessitated a temporary ban on all exports of arms.[23] In the summer of 1864 Vega and Romero found that they could not rely on the leniency of the officials even when the law might permit it. Vega had purchased some prussian muskets and had attempted to ship them from San Francisco. Charles James, the Custom House Collector, had seized the ship-ment and stored it in Cenicia Arsenal. On September 4, 1863, Lincoln had modified the ban on the exportation of arms which had been imported into the United States to allow them to be returned to the port from which they came. Vega applied for permission to send his muskets back to Homberg, from where they could be sent to Mexico. To his surprise, James refused, on the grounds that his interpretation of the law was that the new decree applied only to future imports and not to previous ones.[24]

When the Civil War reached its final stages, the official position of the government underwent a gradual change. The turning point in the arms matter came in late 1865. Major General Irvin McDowel, in command of the Department of the

Pacific, issued General Order No. 17 prohibiting the transportation of arms across the California and Arizona borders into Mexico. This was a major blow to the Mexican government, as most of the ports in Mexico were then closed by the French. When Romero protested to the State Department, his position was upheld by a legal ruling of the Attorney General. Before the decision was made, however, General U. S. Grant already had sent instructions that the order be revoked.[25] Grant at this time was convinced that the United States should take an active part in the expulsion of the French from Mexico. In his memoirs he later recalled:

> Under pretense of protecting their citizens these nations seized upon Mexico as a foothold for establishing a European anarchy upon our continent. . . I, myself, regarded this as a direct act of war against the United States by the powers engaged, and supposed as a matter of course that the United States would treat it as such when their hands were free to strike.[26]

In May of 1865 General Phillip Sheridan was sent to command an army along the Rio Grande. Under orders from General Grant, the army made a show of force along the river. This use of United States troops gave moral support to the Juarez forces and made the Maximillin forces across the river feel that their position was becoming more and more insecure. This moral aid continued until Seward complained that such actions were hurting his negotiations. Sheridan later said that

> After this, it required the patience of Job to abide the slow and poky methods of our State Department, and, in truth, it was difficult to restrain officers and men from crossing the Rio Grande with hostile purpose.[27]

Even more revealing is the disclosure that

> During the winter and spring of 1866 we continued covertly supplying arms and ammunition to the Liberals--sending as many as 30,000 muskets from Baton Rouge arsenal alone. . . .[28]

This change of opinion came when the American people felt that they should aid Mexico because she was fighting a battle for interests that were held in common by themselves. There were those who had always held this position; indeed the policy of the United States was in theory favorable to Mexico, even if in its actions it had been handcuffed by the Civil War. In California Vega was aided by many Americans. Some had official positions; others had the business connections to help him buy without much ready money. Some of these were Mexicans, but most of them were not. Augustin Alviso offered his services "with all the sincerity of a patriot" and his social and economic standing made those services of value;[29] but much of the actual business transactions were carried out by Vega through Quinten Douglass.[30] The efforts of Romualdo Pacheco, the State Treasurer, have already been mentioned; and Gilberto Torres, an ex-Colonel in the Mexican army in California, then in the employ of the U.S. Corps of Engineers, inspected the muskets and rifles that Vega had purchased in San Francisco.[31] E. F. Beale, the Surveyor General in California, and Thomas Brown, the agent for the Treasure Department in San Francisco were early active supporters of Vega; they tried to use their influence with the Custom House Collector to get the arms of Vega released from the Benicia Arsenal.[32] Brown drew up a plan for raising money in California at the request of General Vega and when sending it stated:

> I know the temper of the American people, and I believe that
> they have determined with singular unanimity that no European despot
> shall have sway on North-American soil. They believe that you are
> fighting not only their battles and yours, but at the same time contri-
> buting to establish good government throughout the world.[33]

Another group that volunteered to support the Juarez government was that tough breed of American adventurer that had jumped into every fight in the western hemisphere. With the Civil War closing, the demand for soldiers in the United States was declining, and the chance of obtaining adventure and fortune in Mexico came as a welcome relief. Some volunteers seemed to be professional military men: J. B. Plunkett had been a captain in the Army of the Potomac and was in the Navy on an ironclad when he volunteered.[34] Thomas Fellows wrote in Spanish to offer the services of himself and friends who were in the California Volunteers-- he had learned to speak Spanish when he served in the armies of Nicaragua, Costa Rica, and New Granada.[35] There was no hesitation in volunteering while still in the Army of the United States. Fellows, an enlisted man, did so; and Montgomery Maze was a Second Lieutenant when he sent his letter to Vega;[36] while a Capt. Flynn offered the services of himself, another captain and about fifty men while they were all still in the Army.[37] Many were out of resources and some asked for advances in funds when they volunteered. W. H. Lewis, who had been a Major in the U.S. Army, applied for command of a regiment in a note scrawled in pencil all over a piece of ruled note paper.[38] S. B. George offered "some of the best Military Talent of the country" but concluded that

> . . . in order to do this it will be necessary to act promptly as many of them are now out of employment and will soon be compelled to engage in other pursuits.[39]

Francisco Warner was applying for the commission of Lt. Colonel, but had to ask for aid from a stranger in order to pay his board bill. Warner repeated a request for advance funds saying if refused

> . . . I shall be obliged to accept aid from another source. I can serve the Imperial party, and they know it, or they would not have offered me money to join them, but nothing would induce me to accept their offer.[40]

Many of the volunteers expected to be formed in the same manner as in the U. S. Army; the organizers expected to receive commissions for their efforts. Companies of "well drilled volunteers"[41] were offered if the organizers could receive "Encouragement from the proper quarter".[42] One company wanted the privilege of serving either in the infantry or cavalry and of choosing the colonel they would serve under.[43] The first considerations asked were simple:

> Will you accept a company of good men? Equip them: Commission their officers. And furnish them with means of transportation to where you may need them.[44]

The problem of supply and equipment was treated lightly by one American. Edward Level felt that many Americans would volunteer if sure of their reception in Mexico. He offered to form a nucleus around which Americans could be gathered. The plan was to equip them by cavalry raids on the French troops. "Maximillian shall be our quartermaster and commissary."[45] Others were more explicit in what they expected from the Mexican government:

> Suppose for instance the monthly pay to be the same as in the United States Service--with a promise of a certain amount of land at the expiration of the term of service in place of a bounty--the duration of service to be eighteen months or longer. The troop to be organized similar to a like branch in our service if possible. . . . Means of transportation should (sic) have to be furnished. . . .[46]

The services of bona fide emmigrants were sought by a decree of Juarez in 1865 offering a bounty of land to foreigners who volunteered to serve in the Mexican army. Land worth $1000 would be given to all enlisted men; $1500 to officers up to the rank of Captain; and $2000 to all senior officers. The land would be in parcels no larger than one quarter of a Mexican league (about one square mile); if more land was due the emmigrant he was to receive another piece of property. [47] This measure offered inducements to those volunteers who said that "we do not seek and will not go as adventurers". [48] A correspondent in Jackson, California, wrote to Vega that the edict brought "much enthusiasm for emmigration" among the Americans. [49] Some of the volunteers were not primarily interested in fighting: two printers asked for information on the inducements that would be offered to "good, steady, sober, young men"; [50] an assistant surgeon at the Presidio of San Francisco offered to emmigrate, offering his services as a doctor; [51] even the services of a war correspondent were offered. [52]

The land bounty attracted many Mexicans and Mexican-Americans in California. Rather than volunteering in companies, they came in small groups. [53] The heads of the patriotic _juntas_ found that the decree was attractive to many of their members. The head of the San Luis Obispo _junta_ reported that he and some twenty-five to thirty others had been seriously thinking of going to Mexico after the issuance of the decree. [54] In Jackson, it was reported that the decree appealed to the Chileans and other Spanish speaking people as well. [55] From Virginia City, Nevada, came the report that "there are in this state many volunteers, Mexicans as well as Americans, who have told me. . . of their wishes to take part in the colonization. . ." [56] The land bounty offered a financial chance to many of the poor Mexicans in California; some, however, even lacked the resources to go to San Francisco to volunteer. The same author reported from Virginia City that

> . . . only a lack of resources for transportation from this place to
> there (San Francisco) is what has stopped a great number of Mexicans
> who earnestly wish to offer their blood for the just cause we are
> defending. The majority of the Mexicans are poor and. . . without
> the resources to travel to that port. . . . [57]

The politics of the Civil War were bound to enter into the negotiations between Vega and the American volunteers. Most of the volunteers were ex-Union soldiers, and some of them insisted that their actions do nothing "to compromise the Government of the United States, or to favor the recognition of the Southern Confederacy." [58] A. D. Rock of Austin, Nevada Territory, showed another attitude. In his first letter in 1864 he describes himself in the following terms:

> I have had active service as commander, and can present ample
> testimonials of honour, integrity and competency to command. . .
> I am an American, by birth a Virginian, 45 years old, a civil
> engineer by profession.[59]

Rock later admitted that his "true and honest reasons for leaving this country and settling in another is to get free from a hateful class of Religious, Political fanatics . . . ." Rock claimed that the southern states were opposed to Maximillin and that southerners who would volunteer would do so in good faith and "without any reference to the late troubles in the United States". Unfortunately, Rock complained, there seemed to be an implied understanding "That none shall be allowed to go to Mexico, except those known to be opposed to the Southern States of our Union. "[60]

The response in California to the decree offering land bounties was sufficient to fill a regiment by May of 1865 with the prospect of at least one more battalion.[61] The complaints that the French consul made in San Francisco finally had their effects on the military authorities. The military commander of the District of California issued the following order:

> So long as we are at peace with France and the Republic of Mexico,
> our neutrality must and shall be preserved in good faith. No recruiting
> rendevous for enlisting men for foreign service will be allowed at any
> place in this state. No bodies of armed men will be permitted to sail
> from San Francisco or any other port on the Coast. . . .[62]

A solution came to General Vega a few days before the issuance of the above order in a native of Sinaloa who volunteered to return to Mexico: Gregorio Lopez knew the route overland.[63] The practice became to form the men at the mouth of the Colorado River in American territory where a ship could deliver the arms and equipment; then they would cross the border into Mexico. It was to stop this practice that General McDowels' General Order No. 17 was issued--with the results that have already been discussed.[64]

By the summer of 1865 public opinion was becoming stronger in California for the Mexican liberal cause. In June of that year a public meeting was held in Sacramento;[65] two days earlier a similar meeting was held in San Francisco where the estimated five to six thousand attending passed the inevitable oratorical resolution that came when more than a dozen Californians got together.[66] When Vega was sued for $2000 forfeit money in a contract for arms that were seized by the military before they could be delivered, a San Francisco newspaper commented on the trial:

> If our Government is not at present able to help the Republic of Mexico,
> in its hour of misfortune, our merchants, at least, ought to show
> their sympathies with the noble cause which she defends, instead of
> augmenting her difficulties. [67]

It was in the Congress of the United States, however, that California public opinion best manifested itself. Senator James A. McDougal, of California, led the fight for a new American policy toward the French in Mexico. It was he that called for information concerning the American policy toward the attempts of the French to buy supplies and of the Mexicans to buy arms in the United States. [68] He called for information on the French attempt to set up a monarchy in Mexico; he led the way in the Senate for a joint resolution on the French occupancy of Mexico. [68] In June of 1864 he proposed that the Senate pass the resolution

> That the people of the United States can never regard with indifference
> the attempt of any European powers to overthrow by force, or to sup-
> plant by fraud, the institutions of any republican government on the
> western continent; and that they will view with extreme jealousy, as
> menacing to the peace and independence of their own country, the efforts
> of any such power to obtain for monarchial governments, sustained by
> foreign military force, in close proximity to the United States. [69]

The result was that by this time the Congress was willing to take a much stronger stand than that of the administration and the Secretary of State. The joint resolution on the French occupancy of Mexico, passed in early 1864, hampered the negotiations of the State Department; the Minister to France was instructed to explain to the French government that the resolutions of the Congress were merely advice to the President, who had the power to determine the foreign policy of the United States. When the House of Representatives heard of this they passed a unanimous resolution

> The Congress has a constitutional right to an authoritative voice in
> declaring and prescribing the foreign policy of the United States. . .
> and it is the constitutional duty of the President to respect that policy
> . . . and each proposition while pending and undetermined is not a
> fit topic of diplomatic explanation to any foreign power. [70]

The activities in Congress point out one of the major characteristics of the public opinion favoring Mexico: the main leadership for that opinion came from the Republican party. In the years 1861 and 1862 the Democrats under the leadership of Clement L. Vallandigham and Samuel S. Cox, both of Ohio, used the affairs in Mexico to discredit the administration policies.[71] Although Senator McDougal, of California, was a Democrat, his replacement was a Douglass Democrat who later turned Union Republican.[72] From 1863 on, the leadership in trying to formulate a new Mexican policy was to come from the Republicans led by Benjamin F. Wade of Ohio, in the Senate and H. Winter Davis of Maryland, Robert T. Vanhorn of Missouri, Schuyler Colfax of Indiana, and others in the House.[73] In the election of 1864 both the Radical Republican and Republican conventions adopted platforms that favored the Juarez government against the French.[74] In California the Republicans were Vega's main American support. Romualdo Pacheco and Thomas Brown, active supporters in California, held offices as Republicans. Brown was a personal friend of Major General James A. Garfield, who had just been elected to Congress when he visited California; Brown wrote for an interview with Vega for Garfield.[75] A. J. Bryant, the Chairman of the Union State Central Committee, opened a "Monroe Doctrine" public meeting that advocated more active support to Mexico;[76] previously he had sent volunteers for the Mexican army to Vega.[77] La Voz de Mejico was completely a Republican paper. In 1863 it published a letter signed "A True American" which accused the Democratic party of favoring the French in Mexico and the Confederates in the South, of robbing Texas from Mexico, of starting the Mexican war and robbing California and New Mexico from Mexico in 1846, and of forcing the Mexican and Californian land owners into litigation to protect their property in California. He concluded with the appeal:

> Patriots awake! Unite your forces with ours to suppress the rebellion of the South and then, with the help of time and the grace of God, we will throw Napoleon out of Mexico.[78]

In 1864 the paper came out for the election of the Union party, carrying such editorials as the one entitled "The Copperhead Party and Its Doctrines".[79] It urged all Hispanic-Americans who had the vote in California to support the Union party.[80]

There were several reasons why this connection between the Juarez Party in Mexico and the Republican Party in the United States should come about. Both fought lengthy wars to establish liberal principles; both recognized in the others' efforts a cause complimentary to their own. The Juarez government expressed concern among themselves over reversals of the Union army in the Civil War, feeling that

We should feel these reversals because the cause that the liberal party in the United States is now defending is sister to our own.[81]

There is perhaps a second reason that is more difficult to pinpoint. Taking into consideration the financial support given to Vega by the Business interests of California and the position in the Republican party that Grant, Garfield, and Colfax-- all supporters of a policy of more aid to the Juarez government--played in the promotion of the business interests of the United States, it is interesting to note that Matias Romero, Mexican Minister to the United States, later played a similar role in promoting the interest of business in Mexico. His daughter married Porfirio Diaz, and her influence has been attributed as the cause of the change from political liberal to economic conservative that took place in that Mexican President. Such a relationship may be only coincidental, but certainly the possibility that these two groups found that they "talked the same language" may have played its part.

Reviewing the activities of the Juarez government commission headed by Placido Vega, it has been seen that he did not receive the help from the Mexicans in California that he expected. General Vega's main needs were money to buy arms and the formation of public opinion to force the United States government to allow him to export those arms. In both those needs he was helped primarily by Americans, especially by the Republican party; to a great extent, the aid he received from Mexican-Americans came from those identified with that party. Even in his incidental mission of accepting volunteers for the Mexican army, the Americans in California led the way. In all these matters the Californian citizens of Mexican descent failed to form a group of opinion radically different from that of their Anglo-Saxon neighbors.

[1] William H. Seward to William L. Dayton, United States Ambassador to France, June 21, 1862 in U.S. 37th Congress, 3rd session, House Ex. Doc. 1 (1862), pp. 354-5.

[2] Seward to Charles Francis Adams, United States Ambassador to Great Britain, September 15, 1862 in U.S. 37th Congress, 3rd session, House Ex. Doc. 54 (1862), p. 528.

[3] James Morton Calahan, American Foreign Policy in Mexican Relations (New York: Macmillan, 1932), pp. 278-341 contains a good summary of the U.S. policy.

[4] La Voz de Mejico (San Francisco), August 26, 1862.

[5] Ibid., March 22, 1864.

[6] Thomas Corwin, United States Minister to Mexico, to Seward, August 28, 1862, in U.S. 37th Congress, 3rd session, House Ex. Doc. 54 (1862), p. 37.

[7] Mexican Minister of War and Navy to Placido Vega, July 5, 1863, in Placido Vega, "Coleccion de documentos de la comision confidencial" Vol. III, no. 9 in Bancroft Library, Berkeley, California; and Ibid., September 10, 1863, Vol. I, No. 28. Hereafter the Vega collection will be abbreviated as Vega Mss. Quotations marked (In Spanish) are translated.

[8] (?) Lerdo y Tejada to Vega, March 3, 1864, Vega Mss., Vol. I, No. 43.

[9] Mexican Secretary of State to Vega, July 14, 1864, Vega Mss., Vol. I, No. 6.

[10] Placido Vega Da Cuenta. . . (Tepic: 1867) Vega Mss., Vol. II, No. 402 (In Spanish).

[11] S. Blanco to Vega, June 6, 1865, Vega Mss., Vol. II, No. 402 (In Spanish).

[12] La Voz de Mejico, October 14, 1863, December 24, 1863 and 1864 passim.

[13] Placido Vega Da Cuenta, los.cit.

[14] La Voz de Mejico, August 20, 1863.

[15] Juan de la Fuente to Vega, May 21, 1865, Vega Mss. Vol. II, No. 376; and Donaciono Marzon to Vega, May 16, 1865, Ibid., No. 356.

[16] Mariano S. Vallejo to Vega, September 4, 1865, Vega Mss., Vol. II, No. 496.

[17] Vega to Romualdo Pacheco, November 21, 1864, Vega Mss., Vol. II, No. 24.

[18] Placido Vega Da Cuenta, loc. cit.

[19] Indictment, County Court of San Francisco, California, November 1, 1864, Vega Mss., Vol. I, no. 767.

[20] La Voz de Mejico, August 28, 1862.

[21] Ibid., April 19, 1864 (In Spanish).

[22] Vega to Manuel Rodriguez, October 2, 1863, Vega Mss., Vol. I, no. 180 (In Spanish).

[23] U.S. 37th Congress, 3rd session, Sen. Ex. Doc. 24 (1864).

[24] U.S. 38th Congress, 2nd session, Sen. Ex. Doc. 15 (1865).

[25] U.S. 39th Congress, 2nd session, House Ex. Doc. 73 (1867), pt. II, pp. 221-39.

[26] Ulysses S. Grant, Personal Memoirs of U.S. Grant (New York: Wester, 1896), II, pp. 545-6.

[27] Phillip H. Sheridan, Personal Memoirs of P.H. Sheridan (New York: Wester, 1888), II, pp. 208-17.

[28] Ibid., p. 225-6. Italics have been added.

[29] Augustin Alviso to Vega, August 17, 1864 Vega Mss., Vol. II, No. 591 (In Spanish).

[30] C. M. Radcliff to Quinten Douglass, January 14, 1864, Vega Mss., Vol. I, No. 405.

[31] Mexican Minister of State to Vega, July 7, 1864, Vega Mss., Vol. I, No. 60.

[32] Copies of letters from Thomas Brown to Charles James, July 18, 1864; James to Brown, July 19, 1864; E. F. Beale to James, July 16, 1864; and James to Beale, July 20, 1864; in Vega Mss., Vol. I, no. 536.

[33] Thomas Brown to Vega, June 18, 1864, Vega Mss., Vol. I, No. 493.

[34] Jas. B. Plunket to Vega, June 11, 1865, Vega Mss., Vol. II, No. 407.

[35] Thomas Fellows to Vega, June 2, 1865, Vega Mss., Vol. II, No. 394.

[36] Montgomery Maze to Vega, May 8, 1865, Vega Mss., Vol. II, No. 336.

[37] Capt. C. Flynn to Vega, June 28 and July 10, 1864, Vega Mss., Vol. I, Nos. 526 and 528.

[38] W. H. Lewis to Vega (n. d.), Vega Mss. , Vol. II, No. 345.

[39] S. G. George to Vega, December 9, 1864, Vega Mss. , Vol. II, No. 107.

[40] Francisco Warner to Vega, October 25, 1864, Vega Mss. , Vol. I, No. 735.

[41] E. M. Baylies to Vega, June 1, 1865, Vega Mss. , Vol. II, No. 388.

[42] Charles Cornbloom to Vega, June 9, 1865, Vega Mss. , Vol. II, No. 405.

[43] A. S. Safener to Vega, June 20, 1865, Vega Mss. , Vol. II, No. 415.

[44] Edward Lever to Vega, November 10, 1864, Vega Mss. , Vol. II, No. 118.

[45] Lever to Vega, November 21, 1864, Vega Mss. , Vol. II, No. 25.

[46] Capt. C. Flynn to Vega, July 10, 1864, Vega Mss. , Vol. I, No. 526.

[47] Decree of the Mexican Constitutional Republican Government Inviting American Immigrants. . . (San Francisco: La Voz de Mejico, 1865), Vega Mss. , Vol. I.

[48] Capt. C. Flynn to Vega, June 28, 1864, Vega Mss. , Vol. I, No. 528.

[49] Juan de la Fuente to Vega, May 21, 1865, Vega Mss. , Vol. II, No. 367 (In Spanish).

[50] George B. Shearer and Charles J. Miller to Vega, June 2, 1865, Vega Mss. , Vol. II, No. 393.

[51] A. N. Caswell to Vega, June 20, 1865, Vega Mss. , Vol. II, No. 414.

[52] R. F. Greely to Vega, June 18, 1865, Vega Mss. , Vol. II, No. 413.

[53] Francisco Catala to Antonio Mancillas, May 14, 1865; A. L. Cervantes, May 20, 1865; Miranda Vina, June 5, 1865; in Vega Mss. , Vol. II, Nos. 342, 366 and 397.

[54] Cervantes to Vega, loc. cit.

[55] Juan de la Fuente, loc. cit.

[56] Donaciono Marzon to Vega, May 18, 1865, Vega Mss. , Vol. , II, No. 356 (In Spanish).

[57] Ibid. , (In Spanish).

[58] D. E. Hungerford to Vega, July 16, 1864, Vega Mss. , Vol. I, no. 533.

[59] A. D. Rock to F. F. Gallado, July 14, 1864, Vega Mss. , Vol. I, No. 511.

[60] Rock to Vega, May 31, 1865, Vega Mss., Vol. II, No. 385.

[61] W. H. Servis to Vega, May 14, 1865, Vega Mss., Vol. II, No. 341.

[62] Copy of letter from Brig. Gen. G. Wright, Commanding, District of California, To Col. R. C. Drum, Asst. Adj. Gen., Department of the Pacific, May 16, 1865, in Vega Mss., Vol. II, No. 349.

[63] Crecencio Avalos to Vega, May 14, 1865, Vega Mss., Vol. II, No. 344.

[64] U.S. 39th Congress, 1st session, House Ex., Doc. 73 (1866), pt. II, pp. 221-39.

[65] J. R. Atkins to Vega, June 5 and 8, 1865, Vega Mss., Vol. II, Nos. 398 and 404.

[66] American Flag (San Francisco), June 2, 1865, quoted in U.S. 39th Congress, 1st session, House Ex. Doc. 73 (1866), pt. I, pp. 621-29.

[67] American Flag, March 9, 1865, in Vega Mss., Vol. II, No. 85.

[68] U.S. 37th Congress, 3rd session, Sen. Journal (1863), p. 103.

[69] U.S. 38th Congress, 1st session, Sen.Journal (1864), pp. 246, 374 and 605.

[70] Ibid., House Journal, p. 908.

[71] U.S. 37th Congress, 2nd session, House Journal (1862), pp. 32, 727 and 819; Ibid., 3rd session, p. 111.

[72] U.S. 81st Congress, 2nd session, House Doc. 607, Biographical Directory of the American Congress, 1774-1949 (1950), p. 1011.

[73] U.S. 38th Congress, 1st Session, Sen. Journal (1864), p. 473; Ibid., 2nd session, p. 70; and 37th Congress, 3rd session, House Journal (1862), p. 332; U.S. 38th Congress, 1st session, House Journal (1864), p. 202; U.S. 39th Congress, 1st session, House Journal (1866), p. 40.

[74] Calahan, op. cit., pp. 297-8.

[75] Brown to Feba, April 20, 1865, Vega Mss., Vol. II, No. 315.

[76] American Flag, June 2, 1865, loc. cit.

[77] A. J. Bruant to Vega, May 18, 1865, Vega Mss., Vol. II, No. 361.

[78] La Voz de Mejico, September 1, 1863 (In Spanish).

[79] Ibid., October 13, 1864.

[80]Ibid., October 15, 1864.

[81]Felipe de Arellano to Vega, October 23, 1863, Vega Mss., Vol. I, No. 211 (In Spanish).

CONCLUSION

The first conclusion that should be made concerning the early Mexican assimilation into California society is obvious: the Mexican influence never had a chance to modify greatly that society. From the very beginning, the Mexicans were too busy trying to protect their individual interests from the overwhelming Yankee tide of immigration to be able to present a vigorous defense of their old ways; in the ever-expanding economic conditions during the period from 1850 to 1875 the old Mexican economic ways had little chance against the new Yankee system.

The clash between the two cultures was primarily economic: for southern California--Mexican California--was primarily agricultural, while northern California interests were soon dominated by business and commerce. The view of the Mexicans in the mines, and the passing of the ranchos has shown that these economic issues were never clearly defined on a strict racial basis, however. But because the clashes between the two races were primarily economic, when the economic issues were settled--even if settled unfavorably for the Mexicans--the assimilation of the Mexicans could be greatly accelerated. That the assimilation took place at the cost of so much individual misfortune is lamentable, but it was due as much to the social and economic conditions of the time as to a conscious policy on the part of the Americans.

A third conclusion is even more significant. Despite the Mexican War, despite the economic and social persecution during the gold rush, despite the failure of the Mexican American voters to place in office members of their racial origin, the Mexican Americans failed to develop the "hyphenated-American" consciousness to a degree that was typical of other racial concentrations in the United States. Within a generation the assimilation of the Mexicans in California had, to a great degree, succeeded. From that time on, for the first time, a valid distinction must be made between the Mexicans and the Americans of Mexican descent in California. The importance of this distinction should not be underestimated. The latter were to form a bridge or steppingstone to American society for the forthcoming waves of migration from Mexico. They were to provide the catalyst which would speed the assimilation of future Mexicans in California.

APPENDIX A

A MEXICAN IN THE MINES

A

Translation

of

The Mining Experiences

of

Antonio Franco Coronel

As Described in his Memoir

"Cosas de California"

A

Manuscript

in

Bancroft Library

Berkeley, California

Antonio Franco Coronel was born in 1818 and came to California with his father in 1834. He was granted the Rancho Sierra de los Verdugos in 1846, and although the claim was not upheld by the U.S. Land Commission, he remained an influential and wealthy man even until his death in 1893. Although he took active part in the military operations in southern California against the United States he filled many offices in later years. He was mayor of Los Angeles in 1853, a member of the city council from 1864 to 1867, and state treasurer from 1867 to 1871. In 1877 he dictated the 265 page manuscript for the Bancroft collection. It is the only one of the memoirs in that collection which dwells at any length on the narrator's experiences in the mines. As such the work is important as one of the few source materials in Spanish on that period. The following is a translation of pages 140 to 186 of that work. The punctuation, except for instances of clarity, is the same as in the original.

At the news of the discovery of the gold mines, and the confirmation of the riches uncovered, several parties left from this (the Los Angeles) area. I went in one of them, composed of about thirty men. Among my companions I remember Ramon Carrillo, Narciso Bottello, Dolores Sepulveda, Jose Antonio Machado, Osuna, and various others among whom were several Sonorans.[1]

We went north to the Pueblo of San Jose--there we stayed a few days in order to provide ourselves with food; there we heard news of the discovery of several gold bearing regions. The one that attracted most attention was the Dry Diggins, for which we started out in August of 1848. Upon arrival at the San Joaquin River in the Tulare Valley, we met Father Jose Maria Suarez del Real who was a true vaquero and who had a great deal of gold with him.[2] He told us that he came from Stanislaus Camp--recently discovered--which was a placer rich in gold. We went there and found the camp of some New Mexicans who had left from Los Angeles and who had recently settled there, one or two Americans or foreigners, and several other parties of Spanish people who came from San Jose and other nearby points.

In the center of the main ravine which served as an encampment, I settled with my companions. A little before sunset, there arrived at our camp seven indians, each one with little sacks of gold shaped like a long sausage, from ten to twelve inches long on the average. I was leaning on my saddle and on top of the saddle bags that I was carrying were several ordinary blankets which were used for back clothes for the saddle gear. They were used and dirty and their value when new had been two pesos each. One of the indians took one of them and pointed to the sack filled with gold; he pointed out on it a certain spot as the amount he was offering for the blanket. There was then in that area no way to acquire anything to replace that blanket so I refused the offer of the indians. He increased it in the same manner, lowering the place where he pressed on the sack with his thumb; I refused again. He increased again and then one of my servants asked me why I would not give it to him--that he would make some back clothes of grass.

I took a tin plate that we had and the indian emptied the gold into it and after giving him the blanket I weighed it; there were seven and one quarter ounces--the first gold from the gold mines of California that I obtained. Immediately another indian made the same offer for the other blanket that I had left. I refused two or three offers before I accepted; after giving up the blanket I weighed the gold--a little over nine ounces.

I had brought a sarape from Saltillo for my own use.[3] The indians began to examine it and to make me offers for it. They gathered four of their small bags which altogether contained about three and one half pounds of gold. I refused all offers because that sarape was my main covering. One of my servants--Benito Perez--sold them in the same manner a sarape from New Mexico that had cost him nine pesos and which was a year old for two pounds three ounces of gold.[4]

This Benito Perez was experienced in gold mining and suggested to me that it would be well to follow these indians to find out where they brought the gold from-- to give him a companion and he would follow them. The indians continued buying several other objects by the same system and among the purchases they made was an old horse from a certain Valdez, giving him nearly two pounds of gold. After dark the indians retired from our camp and Benito Perez followed them, accompanied by one of my servants. (One of the mute indians I had with me, named Augustin, whom I had raised as a member of the family. He was one of those brought as

77

children by the expeditions from New Mexico, being captured along the way and traded in California for horses.) They followed them to their rancheria which was not far away; it had been Captain Estanislao's and gave the name to the area. Perez camped on a hill in front of the indian camp and spent the night there waiting for the indians to leave. It was actually the next morning when the seven indians who had visited us left and by climbing some hills headed east. Perez followed them without being seen. At a ravine called Canon del Barro the indians came down and with some wood stakes began to dig and gather gold. Perez went down to where the indians were; they seemed hostile, but he insisted in digging in a place next to theirs and right away he found gold by digging with the knife when he had with him. He gathered three ounces of thick flakes. It already being late, he made sure of the location and that there was plenty of gold, and returned to my camp to report to me all that had happened.

Perez and I agreed to go immediately to take possession of the area without being noticed; but as I had companions I felt that it would be wrong if I didn't give them a share, especially as Perez had informed me that the area was rich and extensive. Probably the news spread like magic and I knew that my movements were being watched. I then ordered Perez and the two mute indians to leave without being seen to take possession of the land which he considered to be the richest. They did so; and when I knew from the information that he had given me that he had gained his objective, I started out at a late hour of night, followed by some of the Spanish people who had been there in the camp.

All marked out a plot of ground, guarding it to begin work the next day. On October 7, 1848, everyone began to work at daybreak. Soon after a little digging we came to the gold deposits and everyone who was working was happy with the results. I, with my two mute indians, recovered by working all day about forty five ounces of coarse gold, not counting the leavings which were in the earth which we saved for washing. Dolores Sepulveda, who was next to my claim, dug up a nugget of a little more than twelve ounces, besides the rest of his gains. All the others, about one hundred and some odd persons, had brilliant results.

The next day I continued on the same job and gather, with my two mutes, thirty eight ounces of coarse gold, not including the dirt I accumulated.

The third day I spent washing the dirt and it yielded fifty one ounces.

The ravine, Canada del Barro, was a thousand varas or more long; from its beginning was where we obtained the results which I have described. From this point it made a break and the ravine made a turn to the south; there was sand bar of about three hundred varas, more or less. At the same time that I was working my claim, a certain Valdez, alias Chapanango, a native California from Santa Barbara, found on the sand bar that I mentioned a deposit of gold which was caused by a large rock located underground in such a manner that it disturbed the path of the current, catching there quantities of gold. Valdes, having dug three feet, found another deposit and gathering it easily, he threw it into a sort of a towel until he could not hold any more by holding the towel by the four corners. Fascinated by his great find, he went about showing it to us, and being satisfied, wished to leave the area.

Lorenzo Soto, [5] of San Diego, of whom I have had occasion to speak elsewhere in these memoirs, was looking around for a claim and seeing that Valdes was not working his, offered to buy it. I do not know what he paid for it, but I do know that he took immediate possession. I was located on another claim further up, about twenty yards away, and could see the labors of Lorenzo Soto. My claim contained a blue and white clay, hard as soap, mixed in which the gold was found. It was difficult to wash, but the work was worth the effort. Lorenzo Soto worked about eight days on his claim, and from the amount of gold I saw and from what he told me it weighed, he had taken out fifty two pounds. The claim had reached water, and in this condition he sold it to a certain Machado from San Diego, who also took out much gold from it.

I left my claim to my servants and went to examine around the third bar of the Canada del Barro. There went with me one of the most famous gambusinos among the Sonorans, known by the nickname of "Chino Tirador". We stopped at a spot which we felt was favorable. He marked out an area upstream from the spot where I had stopped; and I marked out the area where I was. He thereupon began to dig and I went to bring one of my servants and the necessary utensils to inspect the area well. "Chino" continued digging and I, with my servant, did the same. At a depth of four feet, we found a deposit of gold next to an underground rock that divided his claim from mine. This was about 9 a.m. He began to gather the gold with a horn spoon and with his hands, throwing it into a wooden bowl and he would clean the dirt by shaking it, or as the Sonorans say, "dry washing" it. He worked at this until 4 p.m., throwing the gold that was cleaned into his straw hat. I was observing the good fortune of this man, because, I with much more effort, had only been able to get six ounces of gold in the same period. The crown of his hat, which was of good size, being filled, he had left a good deal more in the bowl(which was large). This he did and he was hardly able to carry it. He said he was going to the camp and then I asked permission to work his claim. He cheerfully granted it, and the result was that I obtained seventeen ounces in some two hours of work.

"Chino" had gone to the camp with his gold, where it caused a great commotion. He went about offering to sell his gold for silver, which was scarce. He had already sold some part of it to someone when I arrived. He proposed to sell me clean gold at twenty reales (two and one half pesos) per ounce. I bought seventy six ounces at this price; I did not have silver for any more. Other persons there bought the rest at about more or less the same price. But before selling all of it, he found out that there was a foreigner there with a bottle of aguardiente. He went to buy it and offered four or six ounces for it; the offer was refused. He added to the offer until at last, to obtain the bottle, he told the man to take all the gold he wanted. The man accepted and with his two hands took all the gold he could hold in them from the bowl. He put it in a tin plate and give him the bottle, which was not even full. I asked this stranger a little later if he had weighed the gold which "Chino" had given him for the bottle of aguardiente--he told me and several others, with some indifference, that it was just a little, weighing only two pounds!

"Chino" used the silver which he had obtained by selling his gold to set up a monte bank on the ground on a sheet. One must note that he did not have any clothes but a pair of cotton pants and a wool shirt, plus the wool sheet. At ten o'clock that night, or perhaps earlier, "Chino" was drunk from the aguardiente that he had taken, and was without a cent. All his money had been won from him. On the next day he returned to the claim he had left, but during the night many people had worked it, even by candlelight, taking from it great quantities of gold; and when he examined it, it appeared to him that it would not yield enough to compensate for his work. This claim was taken by Felipe Garcia of Los Angeles and in three days he took out about twenty ounces from a pocket he found.

In much the same manner there were many episodes that would take too long to relate.

I abandoned my claim in this area and returned to the one I was working previously. I continued there for about a month--perhaps lacking a few days.

Now at the beginning of winter all the people on the Stanislaus, with very few exceptions, had fairly good amounts of gold accumulated and wanted to leave to spend the winter in the populated areas, because the news was circulated that the snows on the Stanislaus were severe and could keep out the brining·in of food. But the people did not leave because of the news of a band of thieves on the San Joaquin River.

Don Andres Pico had brought a party of Sonorans from Los Angeles whom he had outfitted until arrival to this area on the condition that they pay him in gold at the price that it was then.[7] In order to insure the payment of his money, he had them working together under the supervision and care of a Spaniard named Juan Manso, one of the owners of the Rancho de la Administracion in San Fernando. He had announced the departure of this party for San Jose and when it was verified the majority of the people on the Stanislaus left for San Jose. The Californians had each brought more horses than they needed and on their arrival to the mines had to set them free, or get together and pay a good price to someone to take care of them. But this care was not very well done because horses were always being lost. So it was that on leaving, many did not have horses to make the move. There was a lot of flying around, because many began to take the animals of other, relying on family relations or friendship. The result was, some loosing and some gaining, they left, leaving very few behind.

I had decided to spend the winter there because my claim was very rich. I had enough ground to work with good results for the whole winter if the weather permitted. Preparing to build a house, I received a letter from Don Ramon Carrillo, brought by Jose Antonio Machado and one of the Osunas, inviting me to go to the Northern Mines, where he had a rich location. He said he had at his disposal twenty or more indians and a considerable flock of livestock, and that he wanted me to take charge for half share. Those who brought the letter, who were friends of mine, excited me with their reports and with what Carrillo had said. Along with my servants and Benito Perez, I picked up camp and, accompanied also by Dolores Sepulveda (a brother in law of Ramon Carrillo) and the two bearers of the letter, went North to the place where Carrillo awaited me. Before arriving there, on the

Rio del Norte, (Feather River) I met Juan Padilla on his way back and he told me that Ramon Carrillo had sold all his animals, delivered his indians to another patron and had left for Sonora.[8] Disappointed in this manner, I decided to spend the winter in Sacramento or San Jose. When Padilla heard my resolution he told me he had a good rancho in Sonoma and some fat animals; he proposed that I accompany him there in order to exchange my horses, leaving mine there to rest, and that I could return immediately to the mines. I gave in to his insistance and we left for Sonoma, where we arrived in the middle of December, 1848.

I immediately sent my animals to the rancho of Padilla and began to take inventory of the equipment in order to return to the mines. I was living in one of the houses of General Vallejo on the square, next to where he lived. Because of previous associations I had with Senor Vallejo, he was the first one I saw on my arrival.

At this time there was a company of commedians in Sonoma giving performances in a hall which had been improvised into a theater. Vallejo, Padilla, I and others agreed to go to one of these performances. We did so, and the comedy over, Vallejo invited us to see the hotel that he had just opened, which, according to my memory, had been the property of Don Jacob P. Leese, his brother in law.[9] We arrived at the hotel which was in the same block not far from the theater. On entering, there was a lobby with a bar room and a table at which there were several Americans and foreigners, some playing monte and some watching.

Juan Padilla went to the table to watch, as did a Sonoran known as Carmelo. There also went with them a Californian named Jose de Garcia Feliz. Dolores Sepulveda went to the bar; Vallejo and I went to examine some of the rooms of the hotel, after which we left by the way we had entered.

On leaving the lobby, Vallejo left for home and I remained to join those who had come with me.

I must note that upon my arrival to Sonoma I learned of the critical position of Juan Padilla in that area, due to the hidious acts which he was accused of having committed against American citizens whom he and Ramon Carrillo had held prisoners during the invasion of Sonoma by the Bear Flag Party. For this reason, several friends had advised me to be careful, that something might happen to me, although I was well known and liked by the honest people of the area.

With this knowledge of the situation, I felt it wise to take Padilla from

82

there, telling him of the danger in which he found himself. He said that he only wanted to see the results of a bet which several present, particularly Carmelo, had made. I went to the counter where Sepulveda was to light a cigar; and in a moment the voices of the players rose in quarrel. I had not finished lighting my cigar when there was a commotion and the room was left entirely dark. At that moment someone grabbed me and threw me from the bar into a nearby room with a violent shove, and then locked the door. I was alarmed, naturally, and I began to look for something with which to defend myself in case my life was threatened. I found an iron bar and with that I waited by the door. Inside I could hear the noise of voices and of fighting with chairs and sticks, etc. In a little while everything was still. A negro who was in the cantina struck a light and I opened the door. I do not remember if the one who threw me into the room locked the door and then someone opened it from the outside. I went out, and the first thing I saw was some broken chairs and Padilla stretched out on the floor in the center of the room, unconscious and bathed in blood from many wounds on the head and bruises on the face. Sepulveda was in a corner of the room behind the counter. The perpetrators of this had disappeared. I then sent for my servants to take Padilla to his room, which was next to mine. I sent after a German doctor, known to the wounded man, who gave him the benefit of his professional services—and thanks to his medical skill and my care and sleepless nights, the man escaped with his life. Padilla could not talk for ten or twelve days, and he could not see for fifteen or twenty, because he had his whole face black and blue from the blows he had received and his eyes were closed by the swelling. When he succeeded in opening his eyes, the whites were completely bloodshot. For almost eight days he took no food but liquids which were given to him by a feeding cup. In about a month he could recognize people and recovered consciousness, but crazy— his senses were not right. He was continually raving, and ever so often wanted to tear the bandages from his head. This made us keep a person constantly watching him night and day—either I or my servants, who were the only ones who, in humanity's sake, offered this service. I asked several persons to take care of him, offering to pay them whatever they asked, so I could go to the gold mines, but I could not find any one to do it. I was obligated, then, to stay at Sonoma all winter and at my own expense.

During his illness the agitation against him continued and several nights

Americans and others passed by the door shouting and making hostile demonstrations. But several people, mostly Americans, who esteemed me, used their influence so that no attempt at violence against Padilla would be made while he was under my care. It is to this that I attribute the fact that he was not torn to pieces or that I did not receive any abuses.

Before I had gone to Sonoma with Padilla I had heard of the accusation made against him and Ramon Carrillo, but they were offset by the words of others who denied the truth of the charges. Carrillo and Padilla themselves positively assured me that the charges were calumnies and that they could prove them so.

About the middle of February, as Padilla was recuperated, I went to San Jose by way of San Francisco, because in those days the trip to San Francisco was very difficult. [10]

I arrived in San Francisco a day or two before Washington's Birthday, landing on the beach which was then were Montgomery Street now is.

San Francisco appeared more like a military camp than a business city because there were more tents than houses. One saw a horde of people of all nationalities agitated by the fever of gold, waiting a means of transportation to the mines, and asking people who came from there news of their condition. On disembarking I was invaded by such numbers of people seeking information that my way was blocked. I answered as curtly as possible in order not to find myself involved in long explanations. With difficulty I was able to arrive at the warehouse of Mr. William Howard, where I rested a while. [11]

I began to seek information about loding places, which if not comfortable, were at least safe, and I found some difficulty in finding a place. Some were pointed out to me and going along the street in the direction of the Plaza de Yerba Buena (now Portsmouth Square) I met a German who had been in the regiment of Colonel Stevenson and afterwards stayed in Los Angeles in business. He spoke a little Spanish and on learning what I was looking for, took me to his home where he offered to lodge me, offering me comfort and security.

There was with me a young man named Manuel Serrano; he, I and the German went to the home of the latter, which was on what is now Kearny Street near Telegraph Hill. His shack, for it was nothing else, was built of planks on end--with two rooms below, a half dining room, a kitchen and a loft. I did not like the looks of the place, but night was already falling. One heard the uproar of shots and could see many people of doubtful appearance. For this reason we accepted this loding for the moment, having to say truthfully that the German was very generous and did what he could to settle our fears. I did not distrust him for I had known him as a man of good character in Los Angeles. I saw in all the lower rooms cots and beds against the wall. The German took me up to the loft where he and a friend of his slept. There he prepared a bed for Serrano and me, which although was not very comfortable, was the best that circumstances allowed. We took them and in a short time went to bed.

About two hours later, the German's friend excitedly came up the loft looking for something which I supposed to be some kind of weapon. At this time, in the rooms below there was an altercation. We rose to see what was happening. In the street we heard shouts and huzzahs from the merrymaking or drunkenness. The trouble below was taking major proportions and I told Serrano that it seemed to be more prudent to leave there. However, the ladder had been a hand ladder and they had removed it. The altercation went on in earnest; they began to come to blows, despite the efforts of the owners to stop it. I was afraid that the affair would take a more serious turn and that the people would turn to their weapons; but fortunately the wall, on which the bunk beds were, fell in, beds and all--which made a great clamour. There was a window in the loft which led onto the roof of the kitchen and dining room. Serrano and I left by this means and in the midst of the agitation going on in the street, without trying to determine what had happened in the house, we went to the store of Mr. Howard, where we called until they opened. There we were furnished lodging for the rest of the night, although all the store was filled with lodgers; the counter, tables, floor, all occupied by friends of the house.

The next day I left on a small boat for the Mission of San Jose because I did not have a way to go directly to the Pueblo of the same name quickly enough to settle my affairs. By this route I arrived at the Pueblo. I was there two or three days and had to hurry my departure because the launch, called the Box, of Pedro Sansivain, was leaving for San Francisco. [12] With some trouble, due to a storm we encountered on the trip, we arrived at San Francisco. There I stayed several days and then returned to Sonoma.

After recovering my animals and making all the necessary preparations I began the trip to the gold mines on the second of March.

My destination was the Stanislaus, but in Sacramento I met people who had returned from that area who gave me the news that the Stanislaus was almost entirely overrun by all kinds of nationalities, but especially by Sonorans; and that the claim that I had left in the care of a friend was occupied by William Wolfskill. [13] I was also told that the Dry Diggings were paying well and I went there with my servants and four companions.

Juan Padilla, when I left Sonoma, went to the north. I arrived at the Dry Diggings and began to work on a fairly good claim.

In this gold field there was quite a population of Chileans, Peruvians, Californians, Mexicans, and many Americans, Germans, etc. The campsites were almost separated by nationality. All--some more, some less--were profiting from the fruits of their labor. But then the news went around of the expulsion from the mines of all those who were not American citizens, because it was felt that foreigners did not have the right to exploit the mines.

One Sunday there appeared notices on The Pines and various other places that all those who were not American citizens had to leave the area within twenty-four hours; and those who did not comply would be forced to do so. This was supported by a group of armed men, ready to make good this declaration.

There were a considerable number of people of various nationalities to whom this order to leave applied. They decided to gather on a hill in order to be on the defense in case of attack. The day on which the departure of the foreigners was supposed to take place, and during the next three or four days, both forces remained cautious, but the event did not go beyond shouts, gunshots and drunkenness, and finally everything calmed down and we returned to continue our work, although daily some of the weak were despoiled of their claims by the stronger.

A few days after this agitation calmed down, a Frenchman named Don Augusto and a Spaniard named Louis were seized. I had dealt with these persons and to me they seemed honorable and of fairly good education. Everyone who knew them had formed the same opinion as mine and the apprehension caused much surprise. Some of the most prominent men gathered and commissioned me to determine the cause of the arrests. I went to an American whom I had known in Los Angeles, one Richard, who had been a sergeant in the cavalry. I asked him to investigate for me. He

86

answered immediately that they had been accused by an Irishman (an old man) of having robbed him of four pounds of gold from a place where he has buried it. I told this to my constituents and then, without losing any time, we collected among everyone five pounds of gold to see if by paying, the prisoners would be freed. I went to the one who acted as chief, whose looks were fierce and displeasing. By the means of an interpreter I presented my argument, hoping to vindicate the two men; I told him that they were known as men of good standing, had sufficient money of their own, and had no reason to steal from anyone. And, nevertheless, here were five pounds of gold, one more than the old Irishman had said was stolen. He took the five pounds of gold, said he was going to talk with the committee and told me to return in the afternoon about two or three hours later. Before the appointed hour, we saw armed men moving about. The majority were under the influence of liquor. Then we saw a cart come out with our two unfortunates, who had their arms tied behind their backs. Two men were guarding them on the cart; and after it came a multitude of people--some on foot, some on horseback. On the cart was a poorly written sign in charcoal, or something similar, which said that whoever defended them would meet the same fate. They came to an oak where the execution was to take place, and when the ropes were being placed around their necks the prisoners asked permission to write to their families and settle their affairs. For having made this plea, one was slapped in the face. Then suddenly they started the cart moving and the two poor men were hung.

This act dismayed me and it had the same effect on many others. Two days later I picked up camp and went to the northern mines.

The reason for most of the antipathy against the Spanish race was that the majority of them were Sonorans who were men used to gold mining and consequently more quickly attained better results--as did the Californians by having come first and acquired the same art. Those who came later were possessed with a terrible fever to obtain gold, and could not satisfy it because their labors gave them little or nothing, or because they were not satisfied with what they got. They hoped to become rich in a minute. These, I say, could not resign themselves to patiently see the better fortune of others. Add to this fever, that which comes from excessive use of liquor. Add also that among so many people of some many nationalities there were a great number of dissolute men, capable of all the conceivable crimes; and the circumstances of there being no laws or authorities to protect the rights and lives of men, gave these wicked men an advantage over peaceful and honorable men. Properly speaking, there was no law in those days but that of force; and in the end the decent people had to establish law of retaliation in their own defense.

Having arrived at the mines above the Rio del Norte--the one which empties into the Sacramento, going by Marysville (the Feather River)--while looking for a place to settle, I arrived at a camp where a Spaniard from Los Angeles had a small store for dry goods and meat. I camped nearby to learn of places where I could mine. In the course of the conversation he let me know that he was well satisfied, that he wished to see if someone would buy his place and his business so he could return to Los Angeles. I was convinced that this offered profits and we came to an agreement; I gave him five pounds of gold for goods which today would not cost one hundred pesos; but the profit came in that there was a camp of indians nearby, they were the business of this place. The way that they did business was to throw a little gold in the palm of the hand and point to the object they wished to buy. Even though the quantity of gold which they threw in their hand was very little, it was worth--even then and there--more than double the value of the object, sometimes up to four times as much. The method of buying meat was the following: throwing the gold into the palm of the hand they pointed out on the hanging quarters of meat the part that they wished cut for them. The seller cuts a piece which at his fancy seems to be advantageous. If the indian sees that the meat is too little, he adds more gold, and the seller adds more meat; and these operations continue until both are satisfied.

I took possession of the place; I bought six head of cattle at one hundred pesos a piece and was occupied in this business for about a couple of weeks making me fourteen pounds of gold. As the business seemed to be very profitable I planned to enlarge it. I left my brother there with my servants, going to the Stanislaus River to buy a small team of mules to load them in Sacramento with goods in order to continue my business.

Dolores Sepulveda accompanied me on this expedition. Having arrived at the Stanislaus, I bought ten matched mules and went to Sacramento.

The Stanislaus was not the same as I had left it ten months before, but was already filled with log shacks and tents where there were a great deal of gambling tables. There you saw gold, not as the most precious metal, but as something which did not cost to acquire. You saw men who by their looks nobody would give a cent for in normal times, place on a bet bags of gold each one of which today would insure to a family as much happiness as money can buy. Such was the indifference of the men who lost these sums that the next day they began anew their labors as if they had saved their earnings. No one was stopped by the prices in acquiring something that they needed, but the prices were fabulous.

On the trip from the Rio del Norte (Feather River) to the Stanislaus River at a place about two miles south of Sutter's Mill, night had fallen. We were there for a short while when a party composed of foreigners of various countries arrived. In it was Sisto Berreyesa and a certain Molina, one of the first Sonorans to arrive in California. This party brought under guard some indians: men, women, and children of both sexes. They arrived at my camp and made theirs next to it.

To stop the escape of some of the indians, whom they brought as prisoners, and who numbered about forty men, ten or twelve women, plus five or six children, the men had stretched them out on the ground face up, with their feet toward the center of the circle they formed. They tied all their feet together and guarded them, stopping almost all movement. They were naked, the night was cold and they were allowed no fires. For the women and children a faggot fire was lit which served at the same time to give light for the vigil and to give warmth to the guards. The head of the party came to me asking aid to guard these indians because he had to make an expedition to a nearby place. I told him I could not, under pretext that I had to leave early in the morning. Sisto Berreyesa told me that the expedition was to fall on an indian village which was on the other side of a hill on the American River, to punish them because two Americans had been found dead there, and these deaths had been attributed to them. Early in the morning, while still dark, the party arose, leaving Molina and two others to guard the prisoners, and left for the indian village mentioned. I, out of curiosity, saddled my horse and followed them at a distance to avoid being seen. The party arrived near the indian village and when dawn began to break, they began to shoot into the village. Here there occurred a scene of horror, because the old people, women, children and men--some with bows and arrows, some without--fled in different directions, some even diving into the river. But all were stopped and shot. I could not continue to watch this horrible killing and I returned to my camp. This event happened about the end of March, 1849.

Immediately I prepared to continue my journey. Soon there arrived some men to gather the prisoners laid out on the ground, and as best as I could learn, to join them with others they had captured alive at the indian village. Then they continued towards Sutter's Mill.

I continued my trip and on the way, upon arriving at the Consumnes River, a party of some twenty armed men caught up with us. They passed us, and leaving the road went towards the East; we continued on our way. On coming out on the plain we went to the rancho which as I remember belonged to Mr. Hicks. [14] He had some large fields of wheat and a village of indians at his disposal. But on going to the house we saw several indians fleeing in different directions, and the party which had passed us, chasing and killing those they could catch. To this spectacle I tried not to be a witness. I changed direction and hurried away. The next day I was informed that the atrocity was to such an extent that the indians considering Mr. Hicks' house a place of safety, ran to shelter themselves in it. It was not even respected as the party had broken into the house and brought the indians out to kill them.

The situation was so disgraceful in that era that to kill an indian in cold blood was the same as to hunt a hare or rabbit. These infamies came to the attention of the Military Governor, who came to visit these places in person to put a stop to them.

I arrived at Sacramento with my mules. I loaded them and went to the north where I had left my store in charge of my brother. About fifteen miles north of Sutter's Mill I met my brother and servants and others of the Spanish race fleeing on foot. They informed me that a party of foreigners had made them leave at once, without permitting them to take even their animals, nor anything else. I returned to Sutter's Mill where there was a small village. I had some friends there. My object was to see if I could sell the goods I was carrying in order to leave the mines. I sold the goods to different parties and almost all the mules at such low prices that I lost almost one third of all the gold they cost me; these people took advantage of the situation in which they found me.

There arrived there at that time Juan Manso with some Sonorans, still of the party of Andres Pico. Ramon Carrillo and some other Sonorans also arrived.

During the dilemma of staying or leaving, as I was going to do, a certain Fisher, a merchant of Sutter's Mill and an old friend of mine from Los Angeles, with other merchants of the area, began to persuade me that such a standard was not the feeling of the majority of the people in that area and that those actions must have been done by a party of criminals because it had been made public, and therefore known, that Californians were considered the same as other Americans. They said that they would give us a document signed by the main citizens there in which they would commend us as citizens and worthy of respect. I did not wish to give in, but on the insistence of others, I agreed to return to begin again to mine for gold.

I turned again toward the upper American River along with all the rest who with me formed a party of about forty men. After making explorations in all directions, Benito Perez, my servant, arrived at our camp with some gold, telling us that the area seemed to be rich. The party did not move. The next day I went with Perez to make a more thorough examination of the place where he found the gold. I was convinced that there was enough gold to give the entire party work for two or three weeks.

We settled there; the location was as follows: An island about two thousand yards long and some two hundred wide forming an angle that was in front of a ravine that had been very richly worked by the Bacas, some New Mexicans who lived in Sonoma.

As the inspection that Perez and I made showed, all the length of this island was perhaps one large rock, or perhaps a tier of rocks, which did not show on the surface. The gold was mixed with the rock the entire length of the island in a vein of dirt that was not more than one or two feet wide. The depth varied from three to ten feet and in spots we had to remove a great deal of rock to come to the vein. I was nominated head of the party so we could set up rules which would govern us for our protection. I must note that there was not a single sign of gold on the rest of the island, we examined it completely.

The rules we adopted were: whenever some stranger came, to tell him nothing of our bonanza and if he arrived at a time when we were washing the earth that had the gold in it to stop that work and pretend doing something else; that no one was to go to Sutter's Mill--in the case of need of provisions, only that person of the

91

highest confidence nominated for that purpose.

Among the party of Ramon Carrillo was an Irishman who was long established in California; a good man, but with the defect of being fond of whiskey. I told Carrillo that I was afraid that because of this the Irishman would divulge our secret. Carrillo assured me that I should not worry, for the man was trustworthy.

Thus settled, Carrillo left for Sonoma and we began our work. The first claim, which was about ten yards long and three wide, was occupied by myself and my servants; the second by Manuel Serrano and his brothers; the third by Dolores Sepulveda; the fourth by Jose de Garcia Feliz and the Irishman; the fifth by the people of Ramon Carrillo; and the sixth and two or three more were occupied by other Californians and Sonorans.

After a week of work, we began to wash the gold-bearing earth we had gathered. This was done on Saturday. Everyone was well satisfied with the results, for they had fulfilled our hopes.

During the week of this work, people came daily to inspect our area; they came to us and asked questions. Our answer was that we were testing, but that we had not yet found gold. Feliz and the Irishman had between them gathered more than two pounds of gold during the week; I, with my three servants, had gathered seven pounds and some ounces.

Saturday night the Irishman disappeared with his share of the gold he had gathered. He went to Sutter's Mill, became drunk and revealed all our business, plans, rules, etc. The following Monday we marked out our claims and proceeded immediately to work. The work was harder for the gold was deep and there was a great deal of rock, but on the other hand the gold was coarser and in greater quantity. Almost everyone had to spend the week working his claim to get where the gold was. During this time, there gathered daily more and more armed men seeking information, as before. They were so well informed of our affairs that on Saturday of this week armed men began to drift down and set up their camp next to ours. Immediately I thought what the object of these men was, and cautioned all our party to be very cautious and prudent in order not to give a pretext to the others to bother us.

Everyone was then gathering the earth which was very rich and promised better results than the first week. About 10 a. m. all these envious people, in number over one hundred, invaded our claims at the moment when we were all within

them. The invaders were so courteous, they asked who was the head of our party.
On being pointed out, the head of their party and about eight others came to my claim,
four were already around my claim. All of these men carried pistols on their hips
and bowie knives; some had rifles, and several carried picks and shovels.

The head of their party addressed me--he and two others armed with picks
and shovels coming into my claim. He made me understand that it was his, because
before we had claimed the place, he and his people had taken possession and had set
up claim markers from one side of the river to the other. He told me several other
things in English which I did not understand at the moment, but it all reduced to say
that it was his property. Excited, I answered with some harsh words, but fortunately he did not understand me. Immediately I could reflect that gold was not worth
risking my life in this manner.

The other invaders took possession of the other claims in the same manner.
My companions fled to our camp before me--had armed themselves and I could see
planned hostile actions. They had already sent for the horses to be saddled. I
arrived where they were and persuaded them to be calm, for whatever attempt they
made would be fruitless, and told them, that for me, the gold mines were over.

We mounted our horses and abandoned the place. The party dispersed and
I left for Los Angeles without stopping any place more than was necessary.

Before concluding my story in respect to the gold mines of California, I
wish to add a story which should prove interesting.

One of my servants, Benito Perez, of whom I have previously spoken,
brought with him his wife. When we arrived at the Stanislaus we set aside a half an
ounce of gold daily for her and she was to cook and wash for me and my four servants, which included her husband. Of these four servants, only the two mute
indians remained with me on arrival to the gold mines. The others began to work
on their own with me, owing me only what it had cost me to bring them there.

On making our food she added a little to it and sold the left overs to those
nearby who asked for them. She saw that the business paid well, and she on her own
account bought meat, beans, and other of the more necessary staples and set a price
of one peso for a plate of beans and a wheat tortilla. This business reached such
proportions that she made three or four ounces of gold a day. And for greater
profit, the scales in which she took the gold, which she considered equivilent to one

peso, was made of tin, from a can of Nantes sardines; the balance rod from a stick and the weight from a flattened shot. From which, one can guess, the scale was not very true, and it always leaned in favor of the wife of Benito Perez. Afterwards she lowered her prices, when there was competition; but the result was, on returning from the gold mines to Los Angeles, that is, after two or three months of work, I weighed the gold in my scales, which were accurate, and she had made with that business, the trifling sum of thirteen pounds, seven ounces of gold. [15] This gives an idea, with what I have said before, of the abundance of gold and the insignificant value it had.

[1] Narciso Bottello was born in 1809 in Alamos, Sonora and came to California in 1833. He was granted land at San Juan Capistrano in 1841 and Rancho La Cienega in 1846. He did not file a grant before the land commission and by 1878 was living in poverty.

[2] Jose Maria Suarez del Real was sent as a missionary from Zacatecas College in the year 1833. He was assigned as a priest at Mission Santa Clara. He was involved in trouble over sale of mission lands and the encroachment of settlers. Because of this and his all too well known vices he was recalled in 1852 to Mexico.

[3] Saltillo, the capital of the northeastern Mexican state of Coahuila, has long been famous for its sarapes.

[4] Three and one half pounds of gold at $16 an ounce would be worth $896; two pounds three ounces would be worth $560.

[5] Lorenzo Soto was one of the two successful claimants for the two square league Rancho Los Vallecitos in San Diego County.

[6] Fifty two pounds of gold at $16 an ounce would be worth $14,408.

[7] Andres Pico was born in San Diego in 1810. He was active against the Americans in the Mexican War, leading the Californians at the Battle of San Pasqual and arranging the terms of peace with Fremont at Cohuenga. He was Bring. Gen. of the state militia in 1858 and state senator from 1860-61. He had three claims for land approved by the land commission, although much of his later life was spent in land litigation.

[8] Juan Padilla was born in Mexico in 1824 and first worked as a barber. From 1844-45 he kept a saloon in San Francisco; in 1846 he was granted two ranchos. That year he was head of a party of Californians in the Bear Flag Revolt in the area north of San Francisco.

[9] Jacob P. Leese was born in Ohio in 1809 and came to California in 1833. He became a Mexican citizen in 1836 and entered into business. He was granted several ranchos, and married the sister of General Vallejo against the latter's wishes. He left California in 1865 to return each and returned in 1885. He died in 1892.

[10] This is evidently an error in the narration or in taking the dictation. More probable is the statement "I went to San Jose by way of San Francisco (i.e. by water), because in those days the trip to San Jose (i.e. by land) was very difficult".

[11] William Howard was born in Boston and came to California in 1839. In 1845 he opened a store with Henry Mellus that soon became the leading firm in San Francisco. He retired in 1850 a rich man. After a trip each his health failed and he died in 1856. Howard street in San Francisco was named after him.

[12]Pedro Sansivain was a Frenchman who was born in 1819. He was the grantee of Rancho Canada del Rincon and also a member of the Constitutional Convention. In later years he was a leader in the wine industry.

[13]William Wolfskill, born in Kentucky in 1798, came to California in 1830. By 1842 he had become owner of the Putah creek rancho. He married a Mexican California and was a leader of the wine industry in later years, dying in 1866.

[14]The town of Hicksville now is located where the rancho once stood.

[15]At $16 an ounce this is worth $3930.

MEXICAN-AMERICANS IN ELECTED STATE OFFICES: 1849-1876

GOVERNOR

Romualdo Pacheco: Feb. to Dec. 1875 (Rep.)
As Lt. Gov. , took office when Gov. Booth Elected to U.S. Senate

LT. GOVERNORS

Pablo de la Guerra: As Pres. of Senate, Acting Lt. Gov. , 1860-1862(Dem.)
Romualdo Pacheco: 1871-75(Rep.)

TREASURERS

Romualdo Pacheco: 1863-1867 (Rep.)
Antonio Coronel: 1867-1871 (Dem.)
Jose G. Estudillo: 1875-1880 (Dem.)

STATE SENATORS

	Conv. Com. 1849	Sessions									
		1st 1844-50	2 1851	3 1852	4 1853	5 1854	6 1855	7 1856	8 1857	9 1858	10 1859
	Non-Part	Non-Part	D=10 W=4 I=1	D=26 W=2	D=20 W=7	D=26 W=8	D=26 W=7	D=16 A=16 W=1	D=19 A=11 R=3	D=27 R=5 A=3	D=25 D=5 R=4 I=1
De la Guerra, Antonio				SLO ¢ SN O							
De la Guerra, Pablo	SAN BAR		SLO¢SB W			S.L.O ¢ STA B D					
Pacheco, Romualdo										SLA ¢ STA B	
Pico, Andres											
Sansevaine, Pedro	S.JOSE										

Sessions---Continued

	11 1860	12 1861	13 1862	14 1863	15 1863-4	16 1865-6	17 1867-8	18 1869-70	19 1871-2	20 1873-4	21 1875-6
	D=28 D=5 R=2	D=20 D=10 R=5	R=17 D=16 D=2	U=31 D=5	U=35 D=5	U=31 D=9	U=21 D=19	D=26 R=12 I=2	D=22 R=17 I=1	R=18 D=14 I=8	D=20 I=11 R=6
De la Guerra, Antonio											
De la Guerra, Pablo	SLO ¢ SB										
Pacheco, Romualdo			S.LO. ¢ STA B.								
Pico, Andres	LA SBR¢ SD.										
Sansevaine, Pedro											

Sessions

	Conv. Com. 1849	1 1844-50	2 1851	3 1852	4 1853	5 1854	6 1855	7 1856	8 1857	9 1858	10 1859
	Non-Part.	Non-Part.	D=17 W=18 I=1	D=41 W=21 I=1	D=41 W=22	D=68 W=12	D=42 W=36 I=2	D=23 A=56 I=1	D=61 A=8 R=11	D=66 R=9 A=4 I=1	D=56 D=16 R=8
Carrillo, Jose A.	▬										
Carrillo, Pedro						STA BAR D					
Castro, Estevan									MONT A		
Castro, Manuel								SLO D			
Coronel, Manuel F.											
Covarrubias, Jose M.	S.L.O. D	STA BAR					STA. BAR. D				
Del Valle, Ignacio				L.A. D							
Dominguez, Miguel	L.A										
Escandon, A. G.											
Malarin, Mariano											MONT D
Pacheco, Mariano G.				SLO D							
Pedrorena, Miguel D.	SD										
Pico, Andres				L.A. W						L.A. D	
Pico, Antonio	S. JOSE										
Rodriguez, Jacinto	MONT.										
Sepulveda, Ignacio											
Torres, Manuel											MARIN S
Vallejo, Mariano G.	SONOMA										

Sessions 11 to 21, Years 1860 to 1875-6 are found on the following page

Sessions---Continued

	11	12	13	14	15	16	17	18	19	20	21
	1860	1861	1862	1863	1863-4	1865-6	1867-8	1869-70	1871-2	1873-4	1875-6
	$D_1$70	D=37	R=39	U=63	U=70	U=61	D=52	D=67	R=54	I=34	D=64
	$D_2$8	D=23	D=32	D=10	D=10	D=19	U=28	U=10	D=25	D=27	R=12
	R=2	R=19	D=9	D=7				I=3	I=1	R=19	I=4
		B=1									
Carrillo, Jose A.											
Carrillo, Pedro											
Castro, Estevan					MONT D						
Castro, Manuel				MONT. Du							
Coronel, Manuel F.								LA D			
Covarrubias, Jose M.	STA BAR Du										
Del Valle, Ignacio											
Dominguez, Miguel											
Escandon, A. G.								STA BAR i SLO D		STA BAR SLO D	
Malarin, Mariano	MONT D										
Pacheco, Mariano G.											
Pedrorena, Miguel D.											
Pico, Andres											
Pico, Antonio											
Rodriguez, Jacinto											
Sepulveda, Ignacio					LA. D						
Torres, Manuel											
Vallejo, Mariano G.											

Key to Party Symbols

A = American; B = Bell & Everett; D = Democrat; D_1 = Lecompton DEM. ; D_2 = Ann - Lecompton Dem. ; D_B = Breckinridge Dem; D_D = Douglass Dem. ; Du = Union Dem. , I = Independent; R = Republican; U = Union; W = Whig

From California Blue Book, or, State Roster, 1911.

BIBLIOGRAPHY

A. Manuscripts

Amador, Jose M. "Memorias sobre la Historia de California". Bancroft Library, Berkeley, California.

Berreyesa, Antonio. "Memoria". Bancroft Library, Berkeley, California.

Coronel, Antonio Franco. "Cosas de California". Bancroft Library, Berkeley, California.

Fremont, Jessie Benton and Francis Preston Fremont. "Great Events During the Life of Major General John C. Fremont and of Jessie Benton Fremont". Bancroft Library, Berkeley, California.

Gonzales, Mariano E. "Statement". Bancroft Library, Berkeley, California.

Hyde, George. "Statement of Historical Facts on California". Bancroft Library, Berkeley, California.

Janssens, Augustin. "Vida y Aventuras en California de Don Augustin Janssens". Bancroft Library, Berkeley, California.

Lugo, Jose de Carmen. "Vida de un Ranchero". Bancroft Library, Berkeley, California.

McGowan, Joseph. "Freighting to the Mines in California, 1849-1859". Unpublished Ph. D. thesis, University of California, Berkeley, California.

Pico, J. J. "Acontesimientos". Bancroft Library, Berkeley, California.

Ord, Angusias de la Guerra. "Occurencias en California". Bancroft Library, Berkeley, California.

Sepulveda, Roman D. "Dictation". Bancroft Library, Berkeley, California

Torres, Manuel. "Peripecias de la Vida Californiana". Bancroft Library, Berkeley, California.

Vallejo, Jose Manuel Salvador. "Notas Historicas Sobre California". Bancroft Library, Berkeley, California.

Vallejo, Mariano G. "Documentos para la Historia de California, 1769-1850". Bancroft Library, Berkeley, California. 36 vols.

------- "Historia de California". Bancroft Library, Berkeley, California. 5 vols.

Vega, Placido. "Colecion de Documentos de la Comision Confidencial". Bancroft
       Library, Berkeley, California. 15 vols.

B. Government Documents and Reports.

(Bigler, John). Annual Message of the Governor of California with Accompanying
       Documents; Delivered at the Commencement of the Seventh Session of the
       Legislature, January, 1856. N. P.: B. B. Redding, State Printer, 1855.

Browne, J. Ross. Report on the Mineral Resources of the United States. Washing-
       ton, 1867.

------- -------. Washington, 1868.

(Burnett, Peter H.). Annual Message of the Governor of California Delivered to
       Both Houses of the Legislature, January 7, 1851. (San Jose, 1851).

California Blue Book, or State Roster, 1911. Sacramento, 1913.

Journal of the Senate of the State of California at their First Session Begun and Held
       at Pueblo San Jose on the Fifteenth Day of December, 1849. San Jose, 1850.

Journal of the Senate of the Legislature of the State of California Begun the Fifth Day
       of January, 1852, and Ended on the Fourth Day of May, 1852, at the Cities
       of Vallejo and Sacramento. San Francisco, 1852.

Journal of the Third Session of the Legislature of the State of California, 1852. San
       Francisco, 1852.

(Riley, Bennett). Proclamation to the People of California on the Third Day of June,
       1849, by Governor Bennett Riley. (San Francisco: Grabhorn, 1942.)

Speeches of Mr. Gwin in the Senate of the United States on Private Land Titles in the
       State of California. Washington, 1851.

The Statutes of California Passed at the First Session of the Legislature Begun the
       15th Day of December, 1849, at the city of Pueblo de San Jose. San Jose,
       1850.

The Statutes of California Passed at the Fourth Session of the Legislature Begun on
       the Third Day of January, 1853, and Ended on the Nineteenth Day of May,
       1853, at the Cities of Vallejo and Benicia. San Francisco, 1853.

U. S. 37th Congress. 2nd Session. House Journal.

_____ 3rd Session. House Journal.

U. S. 37th Contress. 3rd Session. Senate Executive Document 24.

---- ---- Senate Executive Document 54.

---- ---- Senate Journal.

U.S. 38th Congress. 1st Session. House Journal.

---- ---- Senate Journal.

---- 2nd Session. Senate Executive Document 15.

---- ---- Senate Journal.

U.S. 39th Congress. 1st Session. House Journal.

---- ---- Senate Executive Document 73. Parts I and II.

U.S. 81st Congress. 2nd Session. House Document 607: Biographical Directory
of the American Congress, 1774-1949.

C. Books.

Allsop, Thomas. California and its Gold Mines. Edited by Robert Allsop. London,
1853.

Atkinson, Fred William. One Hundred Years in Pajaro Valley, From 1769 to 1868.
(Watsonville, California, 1935)

Bancroft, Hubert Howe. History of California. San Francisco, 1884-90. 7 vols.

Beattie, George William and Helen Hunt Beattie. Heritage of the Valley, San Ber-
nardino's First Century. Oakland, California: Biobooks, 1951.

Beckman, Roy C. The Romance of Oakland. (Oakland, Calif., 1932).

Bell, Horace. On the Old West Coast, Being Further Reminiscences of a Ranger.
Edited by Lanier Bartlett. New York, 1932.

Borthwick, J.D. Three Years in California. Edinburgh and London, 1857.

Brackett, Robert W. A History of the Ranchos. San Diego, Calif.: Union Title
Insurance and Trust Co., 1939.

Brewer, William Henry. Up and Down California in 1860-1864, The Journal of
William H. Brewer. Edited by Francis P. Farquhar. New Haven (1931).

Brooks, J. Tywhitt. Four Months Among the Gold-Finders in Alta California:
Being the Diary of an Expedition from San Francisco to the Gold Districts.
New York, 1849.

Browne, J. Ross. Report on the Debates in the Convention of California, on the Formation of the State Constitution, in September and October of 1849. Washington, 1850.

Capron, E. S. History of California, From its Discovery to the Present Time. Boston, 1854.

Callahan, James Morton. American Foreign Policy in Mexican Relations. New York, 1932.

Caughey, John Walton. Gold is the Cornerstone. Berkeley and Los Angeles: University of California Press, 1948.

---- California. 2nd edition. New York: Prentice Hall, 1953.

Cleland, Robert Glass. The Cattle on a Thousand Hills: Southern California, 1850-1870. 2nd edition. San Marino, Calif.: Huntington Library, 1951.

---- A History of California: The American Period. New York, 1928.

Colton, Walter. Three Years in California. New York, 1850.

DeQuille, Dan (William Wright). The Big Bonanza. New York: Knopf, 1947.

Fisher, Anne B. The Salinas; Upside-down River. New York: Farrar and Rinehart, 1945.

George, Henry. Our Land and Land Policy, National and State. Vol. VIII in The Complete Works of Henry George. New York, 1911.

Giffen, Helen S. and Arthur Woodward. The Story of El Tejon. Los Angeles: Dawson's Book Store, 1942.

(Grant, Ulysses S.) Personal Memoirs of U.S. Grant. New York, 1896.

Guinn, James Miller. A History of California; and an Extended History of its Southern Coast Counties. Los Angeles, 1907. 2 vols.

---- A History of the State of California and Biographical Record of its Coast Counties. Chicago, 1904. 2 vols.

---- A History of the State of California and Biographical Record of Oakland and Environs. Los Angeles, 1907. 2 vols.

---- A History of the State of California and Biographical Record of Santa Cruz, San Benito, Monterey, and San Louis Obispo Counties. Chicago, 1903.

---- Historical and Biographical Record of Southern California. Chicago, 1902.

Halley, William. The Centenial Year Book of Alameda County, California. Oakland, Calif., 1876.

Heckindon, J. and W.A. Wilson. Miners and Business Men's Directory. Columbia, California 1856.

History of San Mateo County, California: Including its Geography, Topography, Geology, Climatology and Description. San Francisco, 1883.

Hottell, John S. Mining in the Pacific States of North America. San Francisco, 1861.

Hottell, Theodore Henry. History of California. San Francisco, 1885-89. 4 vols.

Hoffman, Ogden. Report of Land Cases Determined in the United States District Court for the Northern District of California. San Francisco, 1862.

Hurt, Peyton. The Rise and Fall of the "Know-Nothings" in California. San Francisco, 1930.

Kelly, William. A Stroll Through the Diggings of California. Oakland, Calif., Biobooks, 1950.

Lang, Herbert O. A History of Tuolomne County California. San Francisco, 1882.

Lymen, Albert. Journal of a Voyage to California and Life in the Gold Diggings. New York, 1852.

McIlhany, Edward W. Recollections of a '49er. Kansas City, Missouri, 1903.

McWilliams, Carey. North From Mexico, The Spanish Speaking People of the United States. New York: Lippincott, 1949.

Menefee, C.A. Historical and Descriptive Sketch Book of Napa, Sonoma, Lake and Mendocino. Napa City, California, 1873.

Merritt, Frank Clinton. History of Alameda County, California. Chicago, 1928. 2 vols.

Morrow, William W. Spanish and Mexican Private Land Grant Cases. San Francisco, 1923.

(Munro-Frazer, F.P.) History of Contra Costa County, California; Including its Geography, Geology, Topography, Climatology and Description. San Francisco, 1882.

---- History of Marin County, California; Including its Geography, Geology, Topography, and Climatology. San Francisco, 1880.

Paul, Rodman W. California Gold, The Beginning of Mining in the Far West. Cambridge, Mass.: Harvard University Press, 1947.
104

Perez Rosales, Vicente. California Adventure. Translated by Edwin S. Morby and Arturo Torres-Rioseco. San Francisco: California Book Club, 1943.

Purcel, Mae Fisher. History of Contra Costa County. Berkeley, Calif.: Gillick Press, 1940.

Robinson, W. W. Land in California. Berkeley, Calif.: University of California Press, 1948.

Royce, Josiah. California. First Borzei edition. New York: Knopf, 1938.

Shinn, Charles Howard. The Story of the Mine, as Illustrated by the Great Comstock Lode of Nevada. New York, 1903.

(Sheridan, Phillip H.) Personal Memoirs of P. H. Sheridan. New York, 1888.

Taylor, Bayard. El Dorado, or Adventures in the Path of Empire. New York: Knopf, 1949.

Wittenmeyer, L. C. Abstract of Title to the Lands in the Rancho San Ramon, Contra Costa County, California. San Francisco, 1874.

D. Periodicals, Periodical Articles and Pamphlets.

"A los Nativos Californios". Society of California Pioneers Publication, XXIII (1941), pp. 42-3.

"Alocucion que dirije a los hijos del Pais H. H. Haight, Nominado por el Partido Democratico para Gobernador de Estado". N. P., (1867?).

Barrows, H. D. "Governors of California". Historical Society of Southern California Publication, VI (1906), pp. 32-6.

Bowman, Mary M. "California State Division Controversy". Historical Society of Southern California Publication, X, Part III (1913), pp. 75-8.

California Reports

Ellison, William Henry. "The Movement for State Division in California, 1849-1860". Texas State Historical Association Quarterly, XVII (October, 1913), pp. 101-39.

Hottell, John S. "Mexican Land Grants in California". Hutchings' Illustrated California Magazine, 1857-58, part II, pp. 442-8.

Los Angeles News.

Los Angeles Weekly Republican.

Mexico City El Siglo XIX.

"Reflecciones a los Californios e Hispano-Americanos sobre la eleccion presidencial de 1864, por su amigo V. Dartin". San Francisco, n. d.

Sacramento Record Pioneer.

San Diego Union.

San Francisco Alta California.

San Francisco Bulletin.

San Francisco Examiner.

San Francisco La Voz de Mejico.

Sheenan, John Francis Jr. "The Story of the San Pablo Rancho". Overland Monthly, XXIV (July-December 1894), pp. 517-23.